FOUNDATIONS

Your Side, My Side, & The Root

****BY: THE MOST HIGH****

GERARDO SANCHEZ JR.

*******Sunday Mass is a full house here in Scottsdale, AZ. I'm wearing shorts, sandals, a polo hat, and a 20 dollar knock off Allen Iverson jersey with my tattoos showing, inside Saint Bernadette's Catholic Church. I hadn't been to church in years. This was a spur of the moment decision, after the night before having experienced wonderful coincidences and helping others. I felt the Holy Spirit like never before. I had to go to church and I knew, I just knew, I had to be there in those exact clothes. On the way there, there was a voice in my head telling me to put a shirt on, over and over, yelling at me. Nerves were shaking, but I kept calm like I always do under pressure. I knew I could not listen to the screams. Angry voices are not from angels. Was I losing my mind? Was I losing my mind and building a heart?

Here at Saint Bernadette's went right into his sermon almost minutes after I walked in, which was Luke 7:18-35 or Matthew 11:1-19, and he focused on these key phrases of the passage over and over "Why did you come to the desert?" "Why do you come to church? To see fine clothing?" "These are the questions you must answer. Fine clothes are found in palaces not in the House of God." Then he sat down like he was in shock, facing to the side, he was never looking at the crowd until he stood up to preach. I could not believe the coincidence considering my clothing, the large crowd of people, and also because I showed up late. An Allen Iverson jersey in church, but it was his high school version, #3 Bethel, Green with Yellow trim and White Lettering. Bethel means House of God in Hebrew.

The service was beautiful and I made sure everyone around me knew my faith was real because I felt like I had to prove a point, but it was genuine at the same time. I 'killed' the peace be with you's, I'm talking shaking hands with everyone and doing those cool black man jogs into the other rows to say peace be with you with peaceful eye contact. You know those jogs some African-American men do usually after they hear a joke or going to say hi to someone. Hey, Peace All Around! I cried during the music a few times, I heard someone say, "It's a Salvation." They were right, it was. I genuinely have Faith now, it's just been so hard to have it these days and I know many others agree and it all came out openly that day, finally. What a release! I haven't been to church in years. So this is a Spiritual Awakening.

I stayed after, to shake Father Rosa's hand, and I said to him , "Why do you come to church to see fine clothing," and I showed him my clothes in the style of Vanna White from *The Wheel of Fortune.* I then waited for everyone else to talk to him first before the little scene I was about to cause. I followed him from a distance as he went back into his private quarters. I felt like I have been chosen by God at this point. My confidence has sky rocketed, you would have thought Penelope Cruz just asked me to marry her. Not only do I have an intuition, but I can feel it, I can feel it on my skin. I knock and my first line was,

"You know you chose that sermon because of me... what are the odds of someone walking into your church out of nowhere, for the first time, dressed like I am in an Allen Iverson jersey no less, do you know anything about Allen Iverson?"

"Yes I heard he was really turning his life around."

"Noooo, he turned his life around when he was 18! He got into big trouble as a kid but if you watch his career, no one played with more heart than he did and he was also courteous and respectful to everyone he was around, including the referees, and he always thanked God for his life...It's just that His image gave him the wrong reputation because people from the 'Hood' finally had someone to relate to, but he did not act like a gangster, he only looked like a stereotypical gangster. He is only dressing like the people he was always surrounded by. I dress like I am in the mafia sometimes, but I am not! Now, I heard you say your church is having mortgage problems during the collection? Churches should be in Tents! You have to get back to the roots. People should be able to wear whatever they want to church, remember, we were all suppose to be butt-naked! When people have to dress up for church it clouds their thinking because they are now worried about their appearance and they forget why they are coming to church in the first place! It becomes a keeping up with the Joneses thing, you know it does. What are the odds of me coming here on this very day dressed like this for that sermon?"

*Luke 7:18-35 - "Jesus and John the Baptist"
*Matthew 11:1-19 - "Jesus and John the Baptist"

The very next day I'm in the Denver airport and decide out of nowhere that I needed to keep traveling and helping people like I have been the past month since the election. I mean I am doing really good out here healing, I feel like this is my calling, but I need a sign if I'm going to actually do this, even though what happened in church should have been enough. Some nerve on me. So I start repeating this story to the lady at the airlines stand that sells credit cards, she loves it of course, she is of African descent. Everyone I have told this story to in person in the last 24 hours, was really touched, and I told it at least ten times so far. I am so overwhelmed with love from God and love for all that I cannot contain myself. I am completely insane but in complete control. I have confidence again! Whatever vice I had, I did not need anymore, except cigarettes. Damn cigarettes.

I then ask her where she is from and she said she is from Hampton, VA. This is where Allen Iverson is from! This is not just a coincidence! I have to get this credit card and I did. She's never heard of Iverson though, she's been in Denver since the early 90s, but she said her family there has to know him, I said, "Yeah most likely (as I laugh), but you have to tell your family to spread the word over there!" I am so pumped up. I feel like I have solved the world's racial injustices with just this one act. Allen Iverson really is "The Answer." This is delusion of grandeur at its finest, but I am fully self-aware of this. I tell her goodbye while apologizing because I know I am coming off as a complete nutcase, but then all of a sudden I turn around and say in a much calmer way, "You know this election was a complete mockery of the system and" ...... She cuts me off loudly, "OK now I believe you, that was my exact words TODAY on my Facebook post, "*Mockery of the System.*" Absolutely was.

"Give us a king like all the other nations have.' Samuel was very upset and went to the Lord for advice. 'Do as they say' God replied. 'For it is me they are rejecting not you. They don't want me to be there king any longer. Ever since I brought them out of Egypt they have forsaken me and followed other gods, and now they are going to give you the same treatment. Do as they ask, but solemnly warn them about how a king will treat them." (1 Samuel 8:5-90

It all really started for me a month earlier. Election 2016. Trump vs. Hilary. I ignored the race the whole time because like I said, mockery of the system, and I have never voted before anyways. Everyone knows politicians are liars (they have to be sometimes) and yet people still believe in them? Just because someone speaks with poise and confidence does not mean that they are correct. Same for preachers too, and even when they are citing sources, one should be figuring it out for yourselves. I woke up in the middle of the night at about 2:45 AM and went right on Facebook and the first thing I saw was a live feed of Trump walking to the podium to accept the presidency. I felt a little shock, but like I said, I ignored the race the whole time because it was just another charade. Fell back asleep like nothing happened and then I woke up later and was overcome with emotion. Panicking almost. Crying. I made a post that read, "WE DON'T THINK WITH OUR HEARTS."

Then I heard a loud voice in my head say, "He's the Perfect Candidate!" Was this my call? Or am I losing my mind? I then soon deleted the post because people get scared when you show that kind of emotion. True people of Faith do not care for politics, for their laws are not the same as our Real Chairman's Laws. I believe many people voted that day almost against their will. Deep down they did not want to vote and that thought made me cry as well. I am completely aware of myself at this point, but at the same time I am not understanding who I am. This was when I started to help others in anyway I can. God is with me, I know this now... Finally.

***One cannot ignore the signs. You are not crazy. It's only the people around us that make us seem crazy because they're not ready to believe, but they will, everyone does eventually. Synchronicity exists, you just have to want it. Do not look, it will come to you. Just volunteer with all your heart.

TO BE FULLY LOVED BY GOD, ONE MUST ACCEPT THE NECESSARY EVILS THAT HE MAY ARRANGE ACCORDING TO ONE'S DYNAMIC.

I prayed that I could go to *The Crossroads* like the "King of the Delta Blues," Robert Johnson. Get Devil Tested. I prayed as I was in despair, crying, on my knees, hopeless but hopeful, "Please God, I'll do anything, I will work for You for the rest of my life, if You show me proof of You. It's not fair for us, there's so much information out there to disprove You, but I know you're there. Please just show me some Signs and I will work for you, Forever!"

THEN HE DID. Yeah sure, if you go looking for signs you are sure to find them, I get that. But, I know what a real sign is. I understand "*Synchronicity*" by Carl Jung. He explains it all in perfect detail. "Meaningful coincidences which may or may not have any direct relationship." The more unusual they are; the more they should knock your socks off. If you want it hard enough, God will reveal IT to you. God is relentless, as you should be in your righteousness as He will not reveal Himself if you are not living righteous. God knows it is hard to believe in Him considering the condition of the world, but be ready once you figure IT out, you're going to lose your mind and most likely some friends. You are going to be astounded, like no other... I promise. Jesus said in the Greek Gospel of Thomas,

"Let one who seeks not stop seeking until one finds. When one finds, one will be astonished, and having been astonished, one will reign, and having reigned, one will rest."

The signs of the Lord are subtle, they come to you in all ways, that are special to you. He wants you to understand IT though. We need The Root and we need to be able to feel secure in our belief amongst this world of tyranny against God. Also, some believers have ruined the true meaning of God. That is the same reason why Christ and the other prophets and saviors had to clean things up for us. Man always ruins what was once Perfect. Main reason: many do not pick up the books for themselves. ALL THE BOOKS! You can trust me here, to point you towards the exact information necessary to bring light to all ignorance, but Please Check For Yourself. Let it resonate in your own skin in your own reasoning. I am just trying to pave the way for you like John the Baptist did for Jesus. There would be no evil in this world whatsoever if we all just followed THE TRUE LAWS OF THE HEAVENLY FATHER and THE EARTHLY MOTHER. Everyone knows it, but I am talking about the true laws, not the laws from people passed down through generations.

   ***Oh The Mysteries of Faith. Now, before the stories and research begins here let me just start off by saying... Just because The Holy Bible has been tampered with by man -A Little- and does not contain every Truth there was at the time to each historical story, while leaving some key points out because of prejudice; Does Not Mean There Is No Truth In There Still. To combat this, simply read all the apocryphal books that were left out. You can go read every book that has been left out of The Bible now: *The Dead Sea Scrolls* and *The Nag Hammadi Scriptures* featuring such gospels from: Phillip, James, Peter, John, Thomas, Mary, and yes Judas. You will recognize The Truth, because you are here to seek The Truth and The Truth is in Our Hearts. The biggest difference between the books left out of The Bible and ones allowed in... Equality of the Sexes and a focus on Self-Awareness, although The Bible does have a very quick mention of the role of females in Christ's priesthood:

"Not long afterward Jesus began a tour of the nearby cities and villages to preach The Good News and He took his 12 Disciples with him, along with some women He had healed and from whom He had healed and casted out demons. Among them were Mary Magdalene, from whom He had cast out seven demons; Joanna, the wife of Chuza; Herod's business manager, Susanna, and many others who were contributing from their own resources to support Jesus and His Disciples"
(Luke 8:1-3)

(Gospel of Mary 10,1-10)
"Peter said to Mary, 'Sister we know that the Savior loved you more than all the other women. Tell us the words of the Savior that you remember, the things you know that we don't because we haven't heard

them.' Mary responded, 'I will teach you about what is hidden from you.' And she began to speak these words to them..."

(Book of Thomas 138:4-21)
"For those who have not known themselves have known nothing, but those who have known themselves already have acquired knowledge about the depth of the All."

This is the rebuilding of The Tower of Babel because it is time, I Hope. What you will read may seem contradictory to peace, but one must understand that Babel came directly after The Flood, when God wiped out humans because all they seemed to do evil. Which He admitted to be His fault in the first place: "The Lord observed the extent of people's wickednesses and saw that all their thoughts were consistently and totally evil. And the Lord was sorry He ever made humans and it broke his heart" (Genesis 6:5-6).

"At one time the whole world spoke the same language and used the same words. They said, 'Come, Let's build a great city with a tower that reaches to the skies; a monument to -our- greatness! This will bring us together and keep us from scattering all over the world.' But the Lord came down to see the city they were building and said, 'Look! If they can accomplish this when they have just begun to take advantage of their common language and political unity, just think of what they will do later. Nothing will be impossible for them! Come, let's go down and give them different languages. Then they wont be able to understand each other.' In that way, the Lord scattered them all across the earth and that ended the building of the city." (Genesis 11:1-9)

***Foundations: Mine, Yours, and The Holy Spirit's

"Every plant not planted by my Heavenly Father, will be Rooted Up, so Ignore Them." (Matthew 15:13-14)

I've never chosen sides. Like Joey Gallo in the song "Joey" by Bob Dylan, "Always on the outside of whatever side there was, when they asked him why it had to be that way, well the answer was just because."

There is always three sides to every story: Your Side, My Side, and The Truth. I prefer to stay closest to the truth. Both sides are right and both are wrong. I try to eliminate the wrong and stick with what is right. I know what is right because the side I stay with is God's Side, but at times the devil is necessary. We can relate this to Donald Trump. His sin was just greed though, I assure you he is martyring himself and he knew how to get certain votes. He didn't care of your color or sex, it was greed. Now, he is with God. Speaks highly of God all the time, never heard it before from him right? If it wasn't for the frenzy of his election, I would not have woken up as they say. My morals are all from The Gospels. That holds true now, but before the election, it was just my side. I truly felt like a different person the morning after the election. I started to receive everything from everyone. I felt like I was being taken over by a spiritual entity, one that was ready to fight for love and bring light to ignorance, but I was angry and that anger drove me like I have never been driven before.

Many people were terrified, I felt it. After speaking to a black friend at the gym he told me that he was uncomfortable and and frightened. This made me run to the sauna so I could cry. The cause of all this bullshit is ignorance. People for the most part, are ignorant. We all have the information in the world at our fingertips with smartphones, but yet we still find a way to speak without knowing anything about it and taking people's word at face value without questioning anything. Why? Many reasons: laziness, following the crowd, and just wanting to hear what they want to hear and run with that. I am only 32 years old and have made poor decisions in my younger years, but one thing I am not is ignorant. The unbiased approach is the only way to combat ignorance.

The Secret Book of John the Apostle:

"The figure said to me, 'John, John, why are you doubting? Why are you afraid? Aren't you familiar with this figure? Then do not be fainthearted. I am with you always. I Am The Father, I Am the Mother, I Am the Child. I am the incorruptible and the undefiled one."

I went back to my home church in New Jersey and soon found myself in a Bible study at my local pizza place in my hometown. Frank's Pizza witnessed The Passion. I cannot stop "correcting" people at this point, this time it was my fellow Catholics at a Bible study meeting. I bring up the topic of Judas Escariot because I told them that I struggle with it. They then read to me the verses in Matthew 27 and tell me that Judas is not forgiven because he didn't repent or ask God or Jesus for forgiveness because it doesn't say it literally in the Bible. I call complete bullshit in the middle of Frank's Pizza with everyone watching me. They're right, it doesn't say it but you have to look at the context clues. It is so obvious he asked for forgiveness, so much so that he believed he didn't even deserve God so he committed suicide- cannot prove that, but it makes sense to me.

~Now I'm standing up, and all the employees are all watching me...
And I start walking back n forth quickly~

"You don't walk from point A to point B with nothing in your mind, saying nothing to yourself, before you kill yourself, after you've given up the person you believe to be the Son of God. He clearly had deep remorse, it says it right here, he was 'Filled with remorse and said that he sinned and then hung himself.' You mean to tell me that he said nothing in-between? If a tree in the forest falls does it make a sound?! So he just robotically walked over to hang himself or was laughing about it? Come on. Second of all We needed Judas to give up Jesus in order for our sins to be forgiven. Does Jesus die without Judas Escariot? Third. It was prophesied that this would happen too! So how was this a complete betrayal if it was suppose to happen?"

What really made Judas do this? Did he have control over it? We are dealing with the Apostles, those closest to the Son of God. If there was any possibility at all for Divine Intervention wouldn't it be for Jesus and His Disciples? So did Judas really have control over this?

"Brothers it was necessary for the scriptures to be fulfilled concerning Judas. This was predicted long ago by The Holy Spirit, speaking through King David. Judas was one of us! Chosen to share in the ministry with us." (Acts 1:16-17)

"Jesus said, 'The Truth is, one of you will betray me. It is the one to whom I give the bread dipped in sauce.' And when He had dipped it, He gave it to Judas. As soon as Judas ate the bread, Satan entered into him. Then Jesus told him, 'Hurry. Do it now." (John 13: 21-27)

It Ain't Necessarily So - Bobby Darin

We have free will, I understand that, but does angelic and demonic possession exist also? There is much evidence to affirm this. Just this past December of 2016, the New York Post, from journalist Linda Massarella, stated that there is dire need for more exorcists after reporting about the October meeting of 400 Catholic leaders in Rome on the subject of how to recruit more exorcists. Of course the newspapers aren't going to report these incidences so why would you believe it exists? Look up exorcisms and you are sure to find many cases. I see it now, that Judas giving up Jesus *very well could be* an ultimate sacrifice! Tarnishing your name for all eternity for the sake of humanity... Thanks to God. What do you think?

The lost *Gospel of Judas* is found in the Nag Hammadi Scriptures and it is not proven where it's from or who wrote it (like many Gospels) but in it, it says Jesus told Judas to give Him up because Judas was the wisest of all the apostles and was chosen by Jesus to hear the true teachings of the Kingdom, and that if he sacrificed himself he would be standing next to the Most High in Heaven for this. That makes sense too, but can we trust that gospel because Jesus did say that "Who betrays me it is better that they would have never been born" (Matthew 26:24). Or, was that a part of the whole "act?" Jesus told Judas in the Gospel of Judas,

"You shall be cursed for generations. You will then come to rule over them, you will exceed all of them, for you will sacrifice the man that clothes me."

This -could- explain the gumption Judas had to give Jesus that kiss of betrayal. Judas could have chosen any other way to point out Jesus to the armed guards, so why a kiss? "Greetings Teacher" (Matthew 26:49). If this were to be true, like I said, this does not mean Jesus was not a Son of God; It could mean we all could be Christ if we are worthy of the task. Jesus said,

"I Assure You, If You Have Faith and Do Not Doubt, You Can Even Say to this Mountain, 'May God Lift You Up and Throw You into the Sea' and It Will Happen, If You Believe."
(Matthew 21:21)

There is such a thing called The Emanation Doctrine, which was thrown away by the earliest churches, which we will get to who. The Emanation Doctrine carries Christ-Consciousness to those who are deemed worthy by The Most High.

Jesus called his shots. When Jesus and every other prophet of all the religions of the world fulfilled prophecies, they weren't manipulating the book or doing it to prove a point or deceive people into thinking they are "The Ones." They were calling their shots. They just started to believe that they were truly chosen... to be *like Gods on earth, and then they started calling their shots! But, none of them called more shots than Jesus, as far as we know. Jesus claimed to be Son of God and died a criminal's death.

When you approach anything with a bias, you will only see it how you want to... every time. This, obviously, can keep you from seeing The Truth. That's the Ever-Famous , Benefit of the Doubt. I have struggled with the Divinity of Jesus. I always gave him the benefit of the doubt though, until I got older and learned much more information and let others tell me what to believe. Could it be that it was just a big "white lie?" But why lie? Was he crazy? Is He the True Son of God or a Prophet? Did He even exist? He existed. Two historians, non-"Christians" Josephus and Tacitus, wrote about Jesus. One must realize that he is not going to get publicity like a King! He was an underground Preacher. There were Prophets all over back then and many were false. You're just not going to get media coverage like a King would! Everyone walked everywhere, there was no internet or TV, villages were separated by many miles, and you didn't have hundreds of ways to get news coverage. To even get the kind of coverage Jesus did with Josephus and Tacitus is a miracle in itself.

My "favorite" is when people say Jesus was just a raving lunatic. If this was true, He sure knew what He was doing didn't He? All it took was 3 years of preaching and then some hard work from the Apostles, which they were all eventually killed for; for just spreading The Word (The Book of Acts). Luckily, nowadays they just call you crazy or just lost and lonely.

This is nothing against the Jewish Religion! I Love the Hebrew people, absolutely adore every Hebrew! True Hebrews know all about real peace! Why would Jesus lie? You know He loved every Prophet from The Old Testament and you know they loved Him too. They could not wait for Jesus to come! So, why would Jesus lie? The Messiah never came?

On Jesus being the Son of God... It was either, "A Big White-Lie" or we have to take His Word for it, because isn't it against the rules to lie, and why lie about that? Or, was Jesus a new age mystic saying he was "God." We did become "like God" in the Garden coming to know about good and evil (Genesis 3:5). That could have been the root of naming Himself God, but I do not think all the evidence through the Gospels gives us that impression, considering all the miracles He performed that no mortal man could possibly do. Jesus did say, "Is it not written in your law that you are gods" (John 10:34). "I said you are gods, you are all Sons of The Most High (Psalm 82:6). Peter walked on water as well, until he got scared and began to sink a little (Matthew 14:28-30). Who are we to deny the eye witnesses? We believe The Prophets of Old. It all either happened because you have Faith or Maybe it happened. One can never be so sure what happened, but your Faith is rewarded Ten Fold. The Benefit of the Doubt is always necessary and respectful in accordance with Scripture.

"Why do you call it blasphemy when The Holy One who was sent into the world by The Father says, 'I Am The Son of God?' Do not believe me unless I carry out My Father's work. But if I do His work, believe in what I have done, even if you don't believe me. Then you will realize that The Father is in me, and I am in The Father." (John 10:36-38)

If Christ was a "white-lie" He sure knew what He was doing. Look at what happened after His sacrifice... Christianity, right? The gamble sure did pay off, didn't it? There have been other martyrs, but none that led to such a movement. And, if he was just a man, isn't it completely insane to die for what He was saying? Don't you think He knew something no one else did? That is one hell of a white-lie isn't it, to go through all that pain. John the Baptist knew it was for real too, didn't he? Does not the resurrection prove this also? Or was that a "white-lie" too? Isn't it against the rules to lie?

How come Jesus is not accepted as the Son of God in the Jewish religion and why did some Hebrews accept Jesus as the Son of God? It is easy for one side, they believed. While the rest? Well it is written all throughout the Old Testament. Many of their Prophets foretold the coming of the Messiah: Isaiah, Micah, Zechariah, Jeremiah, Daniel, Hosea, Alma, Samuel, Malachi, and more. How would they know if it was truly Him? They did not know know him from Adam (pun intended). Now if the Messiah was predicted by every beloved prophet, is it not blasphemy to ignore them? Blasphemy, the same charge Jesus was tried for. Who was the Messiah then? Are we calling all those chosen prophets liars now? Jesus fulfilled every single one of those prophesies, in detail. Some of those prophecies cannot be fulfilled today. Who is going to take careful notice of someone riding a donkey into a city? They'll just call him a nut and keep walking.

Why else? Pride. Pride from the Pharisees. Jesus was a rebel. He was reforming what was wrong in the temples of His Father's chosen people. Jesus tore them all new ones. Instead of having humility and recognizing The Truth, they were prideful, and told the common people how to think about this apparent Messiah. Leaders telling us how to think and some of us listen.

"Do you realize you have offended the Pharisees by what you just said?"Jesus replied, "Every plant not planted by my Heavenly Father will be *Rooted Up*, so ignore them. They are blind guides leading the blind, and if one blind person guides another, they will both fall into a ditch." (Matthew 12-14)

Why else wouldn't Jesus be accepted?

"A Prophet is honored everywhere except in His hometown and among His family.' He returned to Nazareth and when He taught there everyone was astonished and said, 'Where does He get His wisdom and His miracles? He is just a carpenter's son and we know Mary, his mother, and his brothers: James, Joseph, Simon, and Judas. All His sisters live right here among us. What makes Him so great?' And they were deeply offended and refused to believe in Him. And so He did only a few miracles there because of their unbelief."
(Matthew 13:54-58)

And just one more thing, Sheol, is the after-life for the Jewish people. Sheol is Hades. Hades is the Underworld; it is not Heaven. This is why Jesus Is The Messiah, He Opened The Gates of Eden For All. He death was for our sins, that was the sacrifice and first theorized by Carl Jung, when reading The Bible like literature... Jesus was an apology for God's treatment of Job.

This "argument" is not out of a bias for Christianity. My bias is from unbiased research on my own. Can't have a Bias in this game! God doesn't! God sees all sides because He is all sides. I did not come here with a bias. I never do, but of course it is up to you. If you are of Hebrew descent, I suggest reading *"God's Answer to Job"* by Carl Jung. A theory on the root of God's anger; that God evolves with us and also on His own. God's name is I AM right? Carl Jung theorizes that Jesus is actually "The Burning Bush" (Exodus 3). "*I tell you truly, before Abraham was born, I AM*" (John 8:58) and He incarnated as Jesus because of guilt, for how He treated Job. God evolves too, so says Carl Jung. Job was perhaps God's final straw, thus incarnating as Jesus, in guilt, for our sins and His own...

Jesus said He was going to change the world and He did, and He knew He had to die for it to happen. Why? Because people don't see The Light without Guilt. People are so emotionally guarded it takes drastic measures to bring one back to real life, and it all started at age 30 by turning water into wine.

"And I, Son of Man, feast and drink, and you say, 'He's a glutton and a drunkard, and a friend of the worst sort of sinners!' But Wisdom is justified by all its children" (Luke 7:35).

"I Assure You, of All Who have Lived, None is Greater than John the Baptist. Yet Even the Most Insignificant Man in Heaven is Greater than He Is!" Luke 7:28 ***Humility or John stays on earth to work?
JOHN THE BAPTIST

John is the best host this world has ever seen. There is no Jesus without John. The Messiah cannot just show up out of nowhere. Some people already thought Jesus was insane when He started His preaching at age 30. Christ needed an introduction, but only with True Passion & Vigor, no one will believe the Prophesy of the Savior is finally going to be fulfilled if emotions are kept under control. John screamed The Truth. It's not no big deal! This is the biggest deal in history. Someone had to pave the way.

John the Baptist was imprisoned then and he still would be imprisoned now. When someone knows the real Truth, it is impossible to keep it to yourself. John had so much to get his off chest and he knew he had to pave the way for Christ. The Angel Gabriel told his parents, Zechariah and Elizabeth, before his birth of his mission for baptizing and introducing Jesus. So when John's baptizing began. The power of God was within him and this is way too much for the "government" to handle.

Nowadays, they would sedate you and throw you in a mental hospital and put you on drugs. Back then, they kill you and in John's case, they took his head. This was John's sacrifice. He sacrificed himself for the Truth. Just like you should do for yourself, but you don't have to go into the wilderness and baptize people. Just go into your room and scream your truth and then figure out how to come to terms with that Truth. And, if you read the Gospels, you would see that the Apostles always asked Jesus when they were confused. They did not assume nor tell Him how to think. That is just a lesson in Ignorance and Arrogance. How Not To Be That. It takes practice and in this case, practice literally makes perfect.

HERE IS THE SECRET TO FIGURING OUT THE TRUTH ON YOUR OWN

You know how children keep asking **Why** over and over? With each answer becoming more detailed;

"Daddy, why does the Light turn on when you flick the switch on the wall?"
"Because it closes the circuit and allows the amps to flow to the bulb."
"Why?"
"Because electricity is like water in a hose, it is always running..."
"Why?"
"I don't know because it's freakin Harnessed."

That "I don't know" is your root. It will always be there, but don't let it grow. Chop it down if it grown to be too big, make sure you show discipline when understanding your inner demons. Come to terms with it or it will consume you. That "I don't know" can be hard to figure out because it is usually the hardest to admit. If you are not confused, you are most likely not close to the root depending on your fear of self. Sometimes we are so afraid of what we will find out about ourselves because then we find out we are wrong. What we are most afraid of... is what we are least willing to admit about ourselves. No one likes to be wrong, but in order to be right, we have to be wrong first, right?

You can do this alone, no one knows what you're thinking except for yourself and God. Don't be afraid of the emotion that comes with it! Release the emotion, that's living, why pay someone to do this when you are completely capable of doing this yourself? You don't get Heaven without Hell. ALL problems can be solved by finding the root, but one must chop it down from limb by limb dealing with each issue individually, until finally getting to the root. It really is that simple, but it is hard to face yourself. Then how you fix that Root is personal to each person as far as expressing your emotions goes. Coming to terms with that truth is the goal. That is also only personal to you. How do YOU feel about it? Why do YOU think it happened? No one should be telling you how to feel or think about anything. No one should really tell you anything about your feelings or path in life. Don't let them confuse you.

Now if you do try this and are not finding results, it is most likely because you are afraid of yourself. That is like playing *Jenga*. In Jenga you are really just hoping not to lose. You are picking and choosing the easiest pieces to remove in order to keep the tower up, ignoring the foundation. While this is great for the game, Jenga has to be played differently in your personal life. Remove each piece from top to bottom. One by one. Then when you get to the bottom, you will most likely be troubled, confused, afraid. You are in disbelief because you cannot figure it out, but you need to. Then once you humble yourself to the issue, you will Enter the Kingdom of Heaven.

Medications like Xanax and Anti-Depressants and related pills and drugs exist to keep you from dealing with your truth! Anxiety is just F.E.A.R. (False Evidence Appearing Real). You could have valid points for your fear, but that is all it is. I know I am minimizing it, but you should too. You know you do not like taking pills to control yourself. There are many natural ways of getting healed. Find out why you are afraid. Most likely you have a very creative mind so fear can be easily manifested since it is apart of your imagination. You have to flip it, and turn it to love. Sounds corny, but have love at your root and all is perfect.

Some people like to throw around the term Bi-Polar onto others, not realizing it is them that is causing this back and forth and up and down within them. This is a result of people getting stuck in surroundings they are deep down not comfortable in. It is both parties fault. One side tries to accept it as much as they can until something is triggered and fights break out. Then the other side has full acceptance and can't comprehend their reaction so they point the finger. It is ignorance and a lack of empathy on their part. This can be solved in calmer ways if the one side just comes out with what it is that is -really- bothering them instead of masking it in anger. While the other side needs to have humility as their base emotion while this is taking place, because whatever it is that is bothering them, it sure is important. If it can't be solved, someone has to step it up and go. Chances are the one pointing the finger is actually the "crazy" one. Our feelings are never wrong!

Why was Jesus able to perform miracles? Because the world overall back then believed in God. They relied on God. Now everyone relies on hospitals and medications, and when that happens God loses His power here. It's the Tinker Bell Affect. All your illnesses would be cured with Faith but people ruined it. Even Jesus was not even accepted in his hometown and only performed a few miracles because of their treatment of Him (Matthew 15:53-58). It is not because he was spiteful or didn't want to, it was because of their unbelief and stubbornness.

"How shall I describe this generation? These people are like a group of children playing a game in the public square. They complain to their friends, 'We played weddings songs and you weren't happy, so we played funeral songs, but you weren't sad" (Matthew 11:16-17)

Living in a Material World, this world is so materialistic it's not even a discussion. Overall, authenticity cannot be found, and we are embarrassed to talk about God or even give Him a head nod. Keep breaking the ice... People can live simple lives, but no one is simple. What goes on underneath the surface is a lot more complex than the words that come out of your mouth. Everyone avoids emotion at all costs. Why? Because we are living in a material world, it looks weak. Real weakness is being afraid of yourself and being afraid of what the others might say if you call them out on something that has bothered you. The other person calls you crazy or what not at first-- what a genius comeback right? How often does this happen? Then what you should do, instead of thinking you're crazy, is just keep digging away, keep calling them on their shit, and then they react. Who was crazy? The real crazy person is the one that avoids. ALWAYS. They've gone so far from their real truth. It's a cloak of bullshit, just gross. Men do this to men, women to women, and in some relationships. Everyone is built with the absolute truth inside them, it is the dynamics of the world itself that has made us stray so far from it. Medication only prolongs the truth!

You especially don't need these medications if it's trauma based. You're not crazy you've just been traumatized! Learn the lessons from it. You're soul is here to grow! There's no growing in Heaven because there is no time and everything is perfect. On Earth you are given lessons for your soul. You can work out your problems in your room, no one knows you like you! Let your emotions out, just know your audience. We -only- release good emotions, but we mask the bad. Why? Did you know this is the most unhealthy thing for your mind, body, and soul. It is a process, do not be afraid of yourself, or would you rather have a dependency that will lead to health problems and a withdrawal loaded with high emotions. This goes for weed too, I used to smoke a lot and I let it become a dependency at one point so now just a little wine chased by water here and there. Mary Jane IS a natural thing though, and should be used in moderation like alcohol. If that is your thing.

"And I, the Son of Man, feast and drink and you say, 'He's a glutton drunkard and a friend of sinners,' But those who are wise will always be justified!" (Luke 7:34)

God wants us to have fun! Keep it clean though and stay within the lines. You know damn well hard chemical drugs hurt your mind, body, and soul. Cleanliness is next to Godliness. Drugs, weed, booze, medications; they all numb your heart and your sight. Yes even weed, when it is abused.

"So if your eye causes you to Lust, gouge it out and throw it away, it is better for you to lose one part of your body than for your whole body to be thrown into hell" (Matthew 5:29)

I know how hard it is to give up a dependency , I've been smoking cigarettes since high school. I am also scared of quitting now. I am slowly pumping myself up to do it, can't make that promise yet. But, If you are ready to stop the Pills or whatever your dependency is, you might need a detox, or just take a few days off and deal with it, but don't go anywhere, you may scare some people. This is why John the Baptist chose the desert for his teachings. John had more emotions than you could ever imagine. That's one reason why they locked him up and eventually beheaded him, and of course calling out the adulterer King and his brother's wife. Baptized way too many people as well. You already know he Baptized Christ. He spoke the TRUTH with too much passion.

A.D.D. can simply be fixed by multi-tasking, pursuing what you truly love, exercise, and vitamins. Those with attention problems are too smart. I speak from having it myself. We analyze so much in so little time that we sometimes cannot even talk about it without looking like a maniac because we talk so fast or we cannot say much at all. Or, when someone is talking to us we notice all the intricacies about their way of speaking instead of listening to the words. We need to learn how to be fully aware of ourselves before someone is speaking to us. Be conscious. You are intelligent, you just have a hard time giving a shit about things you do not love. Did I mention how intelligent Saint John was known to be, aside from having emotional intelligence he was the first known hippie. The first who thought for himself. Highly intelligent. He was a Poet.

Jesus talked to the crowd about John, "Who is this man you went out to see? Did you find him weak as a reed, moved by every breath of wind, or were you expecting to see a man dressed in expensive clothing." (Luke 7:24-25)

"You don't have to write to be a Poet, some people work in gas stations and they are poets" Nobel Prize Winner for Literature Bob Dylan.

Why do awards have to give quotes like this special merit? I should not have even used it, but the award is fresh in my mind. He did not show up to accept the award, although he accepted it graciously by phone. Mr. Dylan will never tell us why he does what he does because he is well aware of how ignorant some people are, because he read Ralph Waldo Emerson,

"People Do Not Seem To Realize That Their Opinion is also a Confession Of Their Own Character!"

Mr. Dylan knows all about faith, and God wants us to put our faith in his words. Dylan's whole career is a Testament to God. Don't believe me? Watch his 60 Minutes interview. He went to the Crossroads and soon made the trip from Minnesota to New York City. He called it destiny,

"It's a feeling you have that you know something about yourself nobody else does, the picture you have in your mind of what you are about... will come true. It's the kind of the thing you kinda have to keep to your own self, because it's a fragile feeling and you put it out there, somebody will kill it, so it's best to keep that all inside."

Just two months after arriving in the city and being turned down by several record companies, he got signed, in just two months. Broke out with "*Blowin' in the Wind*" a song meant to help free Black people from hatred. Little white Jewish boy from Minnesota with a voice that most were annoyed with, made the biggest fuss in the 60s, and they said God had nothing to do with it? Dylan himself said God had everything to do with it when he said, "I made a bargain with the Chief Commander of this world and the world we can't see." He gave the example of God working through him with the writing of "*It's Alright Ma (I'm Only Bleeding)*" which he said he wrote in about five minutes. Listen to the whole song, no man can write that song this quick, and it begins -possibly- with the portrait of Christ's death, "At noon darkness fell across the whole land until 3 o'clock (Matthew 27:45)

"Darkness at the break of noon, shadows even the silver spoon, the handmade blade, the child's balloon, eclipses both the sun and moon, to understand you know too soon, there is no sense in trying."

NO MAN WAS GREATER THAN JOHN THE BAPTIST, YET, EVEN THE MOST INSIGNIFICANT MAN IN HEAVEN IS GREATER THAN JOHN THE BAPTIST Matthew 11:11

Jesus and John were cousins. John was born 6 months before Jesus and died 6 months before Jesus. And, it was the Archangel Gabriel that told the parents of Jesus and John that they were coming. The same Gabriel that brought God's message to the Prophet Muhammad. John also is connected to Islam and that is through the Mandaean Essenes, whom they consider John to be the patriarch of their Sect of Essenes as they still to this day use the same Baptismal Tradition. You can learn more about John the Baptist in the book, **John The Baptist and The Last Gnostics: The Secret History of The Mandaeans** by Andrew Phillip Smith

THE WORLD FAMOUS ARCHANGEL GABRIEL AND THE PROPHET MUHAMMAD

"I am Gabriel, I stand in the Presence of God, and I have been sent to speak to you and to tell you this Good News." (Luke 1:19)

The Archangel Gabriel is God's Messenger and is all about Foundations. Gabriel is "Hebrew, Christian, and Muslim." But remember, there is no such thing as religion in heaven. He helped Daniel understand his visions, founded Christianity by forewarning the parents of Jesus and John, and founded Islam.

Gabriel just had to come down to meet Muhammad, because God chose him to be the Last Messenger for God, to lead mankind out of sin and ignorance into the Light of Truth (sound familiar?). It's always the same reasons why God chooses someone to teach the people. Sin and Ignorance. Before this happened, Muhammad spent lots of time in prayer. He was very upset with the hearts of men and his escape was a mountain cave called Hira where he meditated. God (Allah) saw that Muhammad was *the perfect candidate* so He sent Gabriel. Gabriel said to Muhammad,

"Proclaim! In the name of thy Lord and Cherisher, Who Created man, out of a clot of congealed blood: Proclaim! And thy Lord is Most Bountiful, Who Taught by the Pen, Taught man by which he knew Not.' Muhammad couldn't read and said he could not. Then, Gabriel grasped Muhammad tighter for the second and third time he told him to read, and then he was able to read the 5 Gospels given to him by Gabriel by way of Allah. This was the Foundation of Islam." (Qur'an 96:1-5)

Allah simply means God. God has MANY NAMES. I will get to them. Gabriel is "Our Angel" too. Why can't people just get an understanding of The Roots. Why does man always ruin something that is perfect, just because they are of a different race and culture. Why do we not accept each other's differences?! You know who is genuine and who is not, if you remove your ignorance first. There is always the rule of the few bad apples. Just let people believe! All God wants is for us to believe. When you believe in yourself you're actually praising God you just don't realize it. God is that essence that is everywhere, but that essence is most specially inside you!

"And (We cursed them) for their disbelief... and their boastful claim: Indeed, we have killed the [so-called] Messiah, Jesus, the son of Mary, the messenger of God. And they did not kill him, nor did they crucify him." (Quran 4:156-157)

"Indeed, they are Unbelievers who say, 'God is the Messiah, the Son of Mary.'" (Quran 5:72)

Christians across the world would say well why don't they believe in Jesus then? IT'S BECAUSE WE DIDNT LET THEM... We make wars with each other for centuries, kill each other's families and then say you should Praise Jesus. Islam could have very well accepted Jesus as the Son of God, considering they accept Him as a Prophet. Also, his birth, life and teachings are mentioned in the Qur'an. Yet, Christianity gives no respect to Muhammad at all when the God and Archangel Gabriel did! But, here is The Truth: The Holy Qur'an does claim Jesus to be The Son of God, The Messiah, *""And (We cursed them) for their disbelief... and their boastful claim: Indeed, we have killed the [so-called] Messiah, Jesus, the son of Mary, the messenger of God. And they did not kill him, nor did they crucify him." (Quran 4:156-157).* To reiterate, Jesus is Eternal, His body was simply a vessel. Muhammad calls Jesus The Messiah several times, but like long forgotten truths in The Bible, The Holy Qur'an has them too. This is what people do for their personal agendas to rule.

I do not want to discuss the few bad apples of our recent generations. Not every Muslim is a terrorist, lets get that straight. There is a lot of crazy Christians too, lets get that straight also. The KKK claims to be Christian! The whole point is to stick to the root and the root only! Anything that has happened by Christians or Muslims after the Foundation was set is complete bullshit and I do not want to hear otherwise. Just stop right there if you are trying to argue that because you are wrong. God is the truth; man ruins the truth. This happened on both ends. Point blank, period. So we want to fight and kill each others' families and then say worship our Savior. I don't know about you, but I'd say no.

Well, I Love Allah!!! PRAISE BE TO ALLAH.

"Gabriel said to Muhammad, 'Proclaim! In the name of thy Lord and Cherisher, Who Created man, out of a clot of congealed blood: Proclaim! And thy Lord is Most Bountiful, Who Taught by the Pen, taught man by which he knew not." (Quran 96:1-5)

Earth is where your soul grows, because time exists. Time doesn't exist up in heaven. Life is all about our choices, but man let their choices get the best of them. Got too evil. This is why Noah and The Flood happened. God promised to us to never flood us out again (Genesis 9:11), and then we still didn't straighten up. This is why Prophets existed after the Flood, help guide us on Earth. But, that didn't work either. This is why He sent us His Son here to die for our sins... What will He do next? "I will come as a thief in the night (Revelation 3:3).

Did God make an imperfect world on purpose? He knew we were going to eat the "forbidden fruit." Only God and maybe The Angels know the answer, but this is what it is! I think that this is what it all boils down too: Earth is just a Test, It was a test from the beginning and in the end we get graded. I hope we all pass! We simply have no choice, but to do what we are supposed to do if we want to get on the Dean's List.

The Test of The Garden: Why even plant that tree in the first place; He knew someone was going to eat from it eventually. Hope for the best and prepare for the worst. So since we have knowledge of good and evil, like God (Genesis 2:5), why can't we be smart enough to choose good... if we are like God. Despite what many think, God -can- be really tough on us. It is God that sometimes punishes us. Just how our parents punish us when we have deserved it or needed it. They don't do it because they hate us, they do it because they have to! *Now, imagine being the Father of a whole planet. You would have to think in bigger picture terms. When He has punished a large group, He always saved the good eggs, like the flood with Noah and Babylon with the descendants of Jacob. Because, it's all about Our Choices, but Destiny also exists at the same time. Understand? Jesus could have easily failed in the desert when He was tempted by Satan, but he didn't fail, so His/Our Destiny was manifested! By His Good Choices. It is our choices. One can see this in the passage, going back to Isaiah 14 again which is said to be about the Devil, "Is this the -man- that made the earth tremble? Is this -the king- that demolished the world's greatest cities."

STOP BLAMING GOD FOR OUR CHOICES

Psalms 78:35 "Then they remembered that God (Eloheim) was their rock, and that The Most High (El Elyon) was their Redeemer."

Genesis 1:26 says, "Then God said, Let us make people in OUR image." Who is US? Is God talking about himself and the angels? Considering the angels came before humans. Then why is there no account of the creation of angels? We do know the angels were already here before earth from (Job 38:4-7), as God is telling Job who the boss is because of his arrogance,

"Where were you when I laid the foundations of the earth? Tell me, if you know much. Do you know how its dimensions were determined and who did the surveying? What supports its foundations, and who laid its cornerstone as the morning stars sang together and All the Angels shouted for Joy."

I think it is safe to say we are made out of the image of God and The Angels, but what was Adam actually? Oh the ever so mocked "Rib" of Adam, which begot Eve... (Genesis 1:27),

"God created people in His own image; God patterned THEM after Himself; MALE AND FEMALE He created them. God blessed them and told them, "Multiply and Subdue It. Be masters over the fish and birds and all the animals."

This simply means God is BOTH Male and Female. He created PEOPLE in His image. It does not say God created Him in His image. Nor does it say God created Her in His image. It says THEM and PEOPLE in the image of God. Neither man or woman is separate nor is either more like God than the other, it is written so clear. Woman is just as divine as man. How do you get Woman from a body part of a Man if there was not already a Woman inside that Man? OR, there was a woman present and we will get to that, but first, why the big misunderstanding? Original Sin...

God never gave Adam and Eve a warning of what the Serpent does. And, Adam was with Eve the whole time she was being tempted and he did not stick up for her like a man is supposed to do, nor did he have to eat anything; Adam didn't have to eat it. He could have refused just as much as Eve could have refused. We all know about negative temptations now because of their sins, but remember God planted that tree Himself, and it was right smack in the middle of Eden. Also remember, why plant it in the first place?

The Gospel of Thomas from the Dead Sea Scrolls reads,
"Jesus said to them: 'When you make the two into one and when you make the inside like the outside and the outside like the inside and the above like the below--- that is, to make the male and the female into a single one, so that the male will no longer be male and the female no longer female...then you will enter The Kingdom" (Gospel of Thomas, 22).

"There is no longer Jew or Gentile, slave or free, Male or Female. For you are all Christians, you are One in Christ Jesus" (Galatians 3:28).

Again from The Gospel of Thomas, Peter said to them,
"Mary should leave us, for Females are not worthy of life." Jesus said, "Look I shall guide her to make her male, so that she too may become a living spirit resembling you males. For every Female who makes herself male will enter Heaven's Kingdom"

Women being treated as inferior is because Man, NOT GOD, blamed Original Sin purely on Woman. God didn't forget about Adam, but we did. All we really heard about was Eve's sin, because man has been pointing the finger at woman since Adam told God, "Yes I ate it, but it was the woman you gave me that brought it to me" (Genesis 3:12). God then punishes Eve, "Though your desire will be to control your husband, he will be your master" (Genesis 3:16). These are the reasons why many women don't possess humility in relationships. It's an Ancient Power Struggle. It is in our DNA, it is learned genetics, passed down from generation to generation with God being the start of it because of their sin. God punished Man too, we forget this part right... "Because you listened to your wife and ate the fruit I told you not to eat. I have placed a curse on the ground. All your life you will struggle to scratch a living from it" (Genesis 3:17). So now we are bitter because we have to work to support woman... Just accept the inner sins for this curse to be reversed. Woman, has to go through pain for child birth. Just a confusing punishment isn't it?

All arguments are never solved because no one goes to find The Root. The relationship of man and woman could have went completely different if man did not ruin it. Eve was made to be an equal, a companion* of Adam, not anything lesser, but a companion (Genesis 2:20). Does this not imply that companion means spouse in Genesis 2:20? Adam was married to Eve right? Mary Magdalene was a companion* to Jesus, as it is written in the *Gospel of Philip* from the "Nag Hammadi Scriptures." We all know this story by now though from *The DaVinci Code*-Semantics.

Have you heard of The Essenes? The Children of Light. The secret brother and sisterhood of healers? Equality of the races and gender existed long before you could imagine, because it actually existed. You can find more on essenespirit.com,

"The Essenes (a secret sect of Hebrews that followed Christ) had women as leaders! All the mystic traditions do not treat women as any lesser than man in any sense. Legend has it that Jesus and John the Baptist were also Essenes or had studied with them. Their roots date back to Enoch which would later form the mystery school of the secrets of the universe he passed down to us through Noah which were in Israel, Egypt, and surrounding cities. I will get to Enoch shortly. The Essenes studied all religions; these are true mystics and healers, Essene means healer. They studied all religions believing them to be a different stage in revelation; unknown facts previously hidden which were then brought to light. They were seekers of the light and understood darkness was also within us. You have to overcome the darkness in order to see the light."

Cannot get Heaven without Hell first. Jesus and John being an Essene cannot be confirmed. Some say Jesus and John the Baptist were Essenes: John was a Mandaean of the south near Qumran (*Home of The Dead Sea Scrolls*) and of course The Jordan River where he baptized. They are the last of the Essenes. "A Nazarene" which Jesus was called in Matthew 2:23. Double entendre in hiding because of his home of Nazareth? John was more likely an Essene because he is said to have kept a certain diet like one... As he "Often fasted." While Jesus said, "It is not what you eat that defiles you, but what comes into contact with your heart that defiles you." And, "I, Son of Man, feast and drink and you call me a glutton and a drunkard." Jesus may have studied with or taught the Essenes, but I believe He only belonged to His Father, like He has said over and over. But, in *The Essene Gospel of Peace*, Jesus mentions His Earthly Mother,

"I tell you in very truth, Man is the Son of the Earthly Mother, and from her did the Son of Man receive his whole body. I tell you truly, you are one with the Earthly Mother; she is in you, and you in her. The light of our eyes, the hearing of our ears, both are born of the colours of our earthly mother; which enclose us about, as the waves of the sea a fish, as the eddying air a bird."

"The Light of our Eyes, the Hearing of our Ears, both are born of the Colours and the Sounds of our Earthly Mother."

Who is The Earthly Mother? Is she from earth? Is she from Heaven or the stars and became earthly? Well, there is a beautiful prayer to say to her after you say the Lord's Prayer, says Jesus in The Essene Gospel of Peace, pray to The Earthly Mother, and of course you may translate it to fit your comfort:

"Our Mother which art upon earth, hallowed be thy name. Thy kingdom come, and thy will be done in us as it is in thee. As thou sendest everyday thy Angels, send them to us also. Forgive us our sins as we atone our sins against thee. And lead us not into sickness, but deliver us all from evil, for thine is the earth, the body, and the health. Amen"

Is not equality the Truth of God? Man ruins everything all the time. The Bible would have been written much different if women were treated as equals back then like The Essenes do, but this does not mean The Bible is completely wrong. You have to be able to recognize fairness to determine what is Truth and what is not. If it is not fair, it is not God's doing. Only the genuinely interested and worthy are allowed in the circles of Essenes, so I will respect them and keep their teachings out of this, but if you are interested, the information is out there if you are worthy to be one of them. Though, their roots in the following could bring you towards their Nasarean Way, from essene.org and many others

"In The Nasarean Book of Genesis (that book is titled: Mattanah) we learn that our planet is only one of countless worlds in a vast universe. We learn that long before our planet was created, the Lord Christ and Lady Christ, following the instructions of Jah (God) and Jahlah (Goddess), established a spiritual fellowship called The Christ Family. With branches throughout the universe, The Christ Family is the fellowship of Beings who have joined the mission of Lord Christ and Lady Christ to be Hands of Mercy. Known by various names in various worlds, on Earth The Christ Family established and oversees the Nasarean religion of the Essene Way. The Nasarean religion of the Essene Way was established in the Garden of Eden, and has always continued to exist, though often forced to work behind the scenes due to the violent conditions of this fallen world... It is written that an angel appeared to the ancient Nasarean Essene Jews and told them that, in fulfillment of ancient prophecies, the Lord Christ and Lady Christ would come to earth through them. But first, said the angel to the Nasareans, they must prepare themselves. The angel gave them instructions on how to purify themselves to prepare for the coming of the Lord and Lady. For seven generations the Nasarean Essenes followed the instructions of the angel. And then, in Israel, an Essene woman gave birth to the Lord Christ: Yahshua (Jesus). And the same year, at the Essene encampment in Ethiopia, an Essene woman gave birth to the Lady Christ: Miriam (Mary Magdalene). From this time on, the Nasarean Essene religion has been a form of Christianity, since a Christian is a follower of Christ. Thus, modern Nasarean Essenes, while considering ourselves to be the heirs of authentic Judaism, are Christians because we are followers of Christ. However, we use a different version of the Bible than does mainstream Christianity, and have many different teachings."

Crazy right? This makes more sense to me. Maybe I was an Essene in a past life. So Mary was born in Ethiopia and they call God, Jah, like the Rastafarians. I will get to them later. So if Jesus was not black, His child possibly was. Call it a conspiracy theory all you want, but you are well aware of who is running the show on earth here right... men. We are aware of man's prejudices against gender and color right? Equality is the utmost importance for the Essene, and when you chop it down to its root, it is all about knowing the truth, treating others accordingly. We are living in a world full of Ignorance. Understand where the separation of races and languages came from (The Tower of Babel) and remove your prejudices. This is your way to heaven. Remove the ignorance of original sin from your blood and treat our women as you would yourself.

Being a Catholic first, I understand that there is foolish pride in the church. We are not the "chosen" church. Some, not all, must have forgotten that Pride is a sin. Yes, Saint Peter was chosen to carry on Jesus' church here on earth, but was he Catholic? No, he had no label. If anything he was Hebrew. He just spoke the truth as it pertained to Jesus Christ. The Catholic Church wasn't even established until about 300 years after Jesus died. Constantine made it legal and then 77 years later Theodosius made it the official religion of the Roman Empire. We Think We are Chosen? Saint Peter is Mother Earth's Pope of EVERY Christian Church on Earth.

One major misconception against the Catholic Church is the Council of Nicaea and that they are completely to blame for leaving out certain words and books from The Bible. Who we really need to blame primarily is Justin Martyr, Tertullian, Epiphanius, and last but not least, Irenaeus. I first heard this information from my Archbishop at the Essene Nazarean Church of Mount Carmel, but feel free to do your own research. Nearly 200 years before the Council of Nicaea in 325AD the dirty politics began against the original Christian communities. Their focus were social and political instead of truthful. With all due respect to Lord Jesus, these "leaders" wanted it to stop at Jesus. Jesus was it, He was all we needed to know and that was that. These orthodox leaders resorted to dirty politics to get their way.

They abolished such doctrines as "The Emanation Doctrine." Where there exists a spiritual universe that the physical universe is patterned after, a realm that also has free will. These Emanations were not created by God, but parts of God. Because souls once found their home in heaven, on earth they retain some of that divinity. Emanations, that we are all an extension of God and that the Christ-Spirit exists in and outside of our dimension and can be given to anyone who is deemed worthy by God. Can't have more than One Christ right? That would share power with other religions and churches right? Many original doctrines were thrown away as those leaders began to put together the Gospels of Jesus, primarily Irenaeus, and were deemed heresies and ordered to be extinguished. Hence why we have buried Gospels at Mount Carmel in Israel (Dead Sea Scrolls) and the Nag Hammadi Library in the town of Nag Hammadi in Egypt. Another ancient text, *The Clementine Homilies,* features the future Pope Clement and his relationship with the Apostle Peter. The book also features Peter's Gnosticism/Essene doctrines including Jesus' brother James the Just who was the Bishop of Jerusalem... And of course another important text left out was The Gospel of Peter itself from the Nag Hammadi Library which was ignored and Irenaeus credits Peter for the inspiration to choose Rome for "his bible." Irenaeus the Bishop from Lyon in France, which was also a part of the Roman Empire, chose the Church at Rome to receive "his bible" because he says the Apostles Peter and Paul founded it even though those apostles did not agree with each other much, Peter was an original by way of Christ. In *Against Heresies* Irenaues states,

"Because of its great antiquity, it is with this Church (at Rome) that every church who are from everywhere, must conform... For it is necessary that every church should agree with this church on account of its pre-eminent authority (Book 3, 3:2)

We cannot blame the Council of Nicaea for the abandonment of many truths, for this occurred almost 200 years prior by early Christians. Now, when you have to change a whole way of order there has to be some common ground or else it does not work! Of course we all wish it wasn't this way, but whose fault is that? In the style of Christ, Truly I Say to You, Stubborn people that are too lazy to change. Sometimes we can blame the leaders, but sometimes it is us. This occurred in Rome in 325 AD, there were already prior religious rituals being practiced throughout the whole empire. However, they could not just throw out every prior ritual and celebration when Christ became the official church, or the people would not practice it. They combined pagan rituals like Christmas with early Christian traditions like the written, communion, and disciplines within the church. A ritual has nothing to do with The Truth, your Heart does, thats it! They had to compromise, there always has to be common ground for two different sides to come together or they will never come together. I am a Catholic first, but my loyalty is to The Truth and although certain truths were left out of The Bible, it is not the Catholic's fault, for the truths were already deemed heresies many years prior and had to be hidden. They had to synchronize the ways of the Church of Rome and The First Churches of Christ in to fit the dynamic of the current empire and the individual.

The only reason there are different denominations in every religion; is to cater to different personalities and cultures.

That's it. God wants us to believe in IT and He adapts as we evolve. I think we are getting near the time when the real truth comes out because all the right people aren't involved in church anymore because some of the rules are outdated and stubborn. Pope Francis IS doing a great job at bringing us back to an age of humility in a Catholic Church that has never been known for that -stereotypically-. Too bad some of the people aren't catching on to it. No church is better than the other. There's just going to be faults in all of them because they're a human invention.

Upon my return to church, I went to my home church where I was confirmed and without wasting anytime, I needed to find out if they knew the truth about Islam. This was during my spiritual astonishment. I was out of my mind, but sharp. I asked the deacon if he know how Islam started and he said it was Ishmael son of Abraham. This is true for how the Arabic people were created, but not for Islam itself. As it says in (Genesis 17:20-21) with God speaking to Abraham,

"As for Ishmael, I will bless him also, just as you asked. I will cause him to multiply and become a great nation. Twelve princes will be among his descendants. But my covenant is with Issac, who will be born to you and Sarah about this time next year."

But, this is not how Islam started, as you know it was the Archangel Gabriel by way of God (Allah). The covenant was for Issac not Ishmael, because Issac was full Hebrew, not Ishmael. The Old Testament was all about God's "chosen" people... Israel.

This story can be found in Genesis 16, Abraham's wife Sarah could not have children so she allowed him to sleep with her Egyptian servant Hagar to have a child. Soon Hagar felt contempt for Sarah and Sarah soon started to treat her with disrespect. Hagar ran away and was soon met by an Angel. The Angel's name was not given, but I am willing to bet it was Gabriel! Gabriel brings messages of foundations...

"Return to your mistress and submit to her authority. I will give you more descendants than you can count. You are now pregnant and will give birth to a son. You are to name him Ishmael (which means "God Hears"), for the Lord has heard about your misery. This son of yours will be a wild one, free and untamed as a wild donkey! He will be against everyone, and everyone will be against him. Yes, he will live at odds with the rest of his brothers" (Genesis 9-12).

Sure Ishmael was the daughter of a slave, but does this make his people inferior? No. Remember every son of Abraham was a slave shortly after this. Ishmael was chosen by God, what is more special than that? So this is the root of the battle between Israel and the Arabic people. God made it this way. Why though? We will not know why, but I think that because it is written... We are suppose to recognize that it was indeed God's plan. However, this does not mean we are suppose to keep fighting. We should look at it like, OK since it was foretold this separation was planned, we should come to the understanding that since we are not suppose to be fighting with anyone in the first place, understand this was part of our human evolution, and now since we have evolved, that part of our evolution is to come to the understanding that it is our duty to come out of ignorance on our own! Allah is God. Allah is The Father of Jesus Christ.

What happens when there is separation between people? War. This holds true for your rival high school or college. We are all the same, but because we rival, we war with each other. So, we should ignore everything that happened in-between then and now. God never said to be at war with each other, that is man's fault, but there is a clear separation of the people in Genesis 18,

"Ishmael's descendants were scattered across the country from Havilah to Shur, which is east of Egypt in the direction of Asshur. The clans descended from Ishmael camped close to one another."

Because of this planned separation God much later on found his perfect candidate in Muhammad when the time was right and sent Gabriel to bring him The Truth in order to bring peace. After telling my deacon to look this up multiple times he finally did and his reply was, "Well Muhammad was good for several years but it did not last." And I said, "Because man ruins the root every time! You know the root is the truth because God is the root! We should not be focusing on what man did, that is a complete denial of The Truth! We can be a special church for starting this, we can go to mosques and promote peace because we know The Root, we are not doing anything different than our Pope. Pope Francis is praying at mosques, we are only following him!"

Of course this is not something most do not want to undertake, especially when they would rather hold true to their old school beliefs. It is not all their fault, they grew up in a time where they were only taught what was told to them. There was no internet and they were at the mercy of their priests. That is just the way it was, but there is no excuse for it nowadays, absolutely none! We have every bit of information at our fingertips in seconds, all we have to do is use our fingers. There was a fill in priest at our church of Nigerian descent and I asked him the same questions about Islam and he knew it was Gabriel! So I asked him why he thought people did not know this and he said, "Because they refuse to accept it." See you cannot stereotype a whole group, even Catholics and Muslims.

Remember about the Few Bad Apples. The Catholic

Priests' taking the vow of celibacy has to be the biggest part of the decision to serve God. Some mystic teachings, like The Buddha, suggest that we should remove all desire to become closer to God, but is that not a desire in itself? Yes and No, because God is not human therefore a desire for God is not rooted in human temptation, it is rooted from our soul, but, we are human so we have some needs, and woman was made for us to love. I said make love though, not sex, love. We were built to make love. "Do not lust, even with your mind," said Jesus Christ.

Many future canonized men that took the vow of celibacy had to live as hermits like Saint Augustine. Out of sight, out of mind. Augustine was a player in his younger years. He "Got Around" like 2Pac, but he gave it all up for God. God loves sacrifice. It would have been in the Ten Commandments if sex was not allowed. Jesus would have said something about it too, wouldn't He? I am just sending a message out to all Priests, what your friends in the church don't know won't hurt them! Still can't lie about it, but you are not sinning by being with a woman. A woman's love might save you from falling victim to much worse temptations. If not, I still respect you and others should too. I know my scriptures and I know you do too:

Matthew 19:10-12: "Some are born as eunuchs, some did not marry because of what others done to them, and some choose not to marry for the sake of The Kingdom. Let anyone who can, accept this statement."

You just have an option. Woman IS Divine. The Right Woman IS Divine and I've never had much luck with women, I love too much too fast, but I'm the Best Wing Man Ever...

"Heart like a Gabriel, Pure and White as Ivory... Soul like a Lucifer black and cold like a piece of lead"

Misguided Angel by The Cowboy Junkies

The Book of Enoch: Where the full story of the 200 misguided angels appear? But first, Enoch was one of only two men taken by God before they died on Earth. The other being The Prophet Elijah in (2 Kings 2:11). Enoch was 7 Generations from Adam by way of Seth, Enosh, Kenan, Mahalalel, Jared, Enoch, and Enoch was the great-grandfather of Noah. Enoch's son Methuselah is famous for being the longest living person in the Bible.

> "When Enoch was 65 years old, he begot Methuselah. Enoch walked with God after he begot Methuselah for 300 years, and he had other sons and daughters. Enoch lived 365 years in all. He enjoyed a close relationship with God throughout his life. Then one day he was no longer here, for God took him!" (Genesis 5:21-24)

> "It was by faith that Enoch was taken up to heaven without dying, but before he was taken up, he was approved as pleasing to God." (Hebrews 11:5)

Why would a man with such importance to God like Elijah not be given much attention in The Bible? Enoch is really only mentioned a few times: Genesis 5:21-24, Jude 14-15, and Hebrews 11:5. While Elijah is world famous, although Enoch has gained some fame in recent years on shows such as *Ancient Aliens*. The story of the Fallen can be found in: Genesis 6, "*Origin of the Nephilim*," which is actually from older issues of The Bible, but not in some current issues. What is mentioned in shorter versions of this is that the fallen married the women on earth and had children with them, and those children (Nephilim) became known as heroes and legends considering they had angelic genes and were said to be giants or "giants," heroes of the time, the famous soldiers or artists. The churches left The Book of Enoch out of The Bible, but the Coptic Church has kept Enoch in circulation since its beginnings in 100 AD. The Book of Enoch has one of the most interesting stories in history too, it contains the details of Enoch's tour of the heavens with the Archangel Uriel and the story of the fallen angels on earth, while in The Bible, if one actually reads it, it does not depict an evil fall here. God, The Creator admitted that His Creation, humans were evil before the flood, and here we see how the Fallen (Sons of God) were depicted as better as The Lord said, "My Spirit will not **put up** with humans for such a long time, for they are only mortal flesh and they will live no longer than 120 years" (Genesis 6:3).

The Fallen committed many "evils" here for it was their duty to let us evolve on our own according to The Book of Enoch. The Fallen knew of God's coming judgment upon them and then felt guilty and wanted forgiveness from God... Enoch walked with God, and the fallen petitioned God through Enoch for their forgiveness. God said No, but which God? You remember Psalm 78:35, The Most High, and that was Jesus' Father, as Gabriel said, "He will be known as The Son of The Most High." And, reread Genesis 6:3, "The Angels will not Put Up with humans for long."

Everyone just writes God to encompass everything we cannot see. There's a myriad of angels and spirits and more than One God. There's also a God of The Dead which Jesus calls Satan in The Essene Gospel of Peace. When Jesus is speaking about The Burning Bush, The God of Abraham, Issac, and Jacob in The Story of the Resurrection He says, "He is The God of The Living, not the dead" (Matthew 22:32, Luke 20:38, Mark 12:27). Satan is the God of the Dead, like the Egyptian Osiris or Greek Hades. Hades, which controls the underworld and is also mentioned in Revelation 20:14, "Then Death and Hades were thrown into the lake of fire- this is the second death."

One God was meant to make things easier and so others did not fall into worship of other Gods. It wouldn't be a Commandment to not worship idols or other gods if there weren't other gods right? And, all Angels are Gods, they are direct Sons and Daughters of God. 200 of them fell to help a lost cause, but humans were corrupted since creation, before the garden. Just by having a choice to disobey means there was corruption. If we want to follow Original Sin... It did not make us evil. Nowhere does it say that the apple made us evil! God was just not happy about it so He punished us. The Fruit made us "like gods," that is it, we know good and evil now, like Gods, that is all it says, evil did not come from that tree. Humans were born with sin. 200 Angels Fell to help us. The Creator knew His creation needed help and over much time, it was decided there was no hope and a

Flood was sanctioned. The Fallen were judged for certain teachings they carried out like: the taking of wives, teachings of the enchantments (spells), and the showing of warlike ways. They were sentenced to wander the earth forever. They also showed us good things: writing and reading, body armor, mining, enchantments, planetary movements, astrology, and many other secrets. So not everything they showed us was actually evil according to God's judgment, like Astrology.

"Do not rely on mediums and psychics for they will defile you. I the Lord, am your God." (Leviticus 19:31)

Keyword *Rely. You still have to believe in yourself and have faith in God. Relying on someone other than God and yourself is what defiles you. Psychics and mediums are here to help the unfaithful, but it is up to you to keep the faith and it is up to them to remind you that God is present in these readings. These people were given gifts for a reason and just like prophets, there are false psychics too. The best ones do not charge a dime! They do it out of the kindness of their hearts. Who controls the answers of earth, controls the power. Remember Enoch was the Great Grandfather of Noah. Noah the grandfather of us all. This is how the secrets of the Universe stuck around, I would imagine, considering it was Noah that stayed. Some also say the Fallen and Nephilim survived the flood somehow, which makes sense considering all the evils that also stuck around, but where did they hide? C'e La Luna Mezzo Mare? Under the ground. Also, their Spirits were said to wander the earth forever. Why? Well, they fell to help, so stay and help. It is just not what everyone has been saying. Read all of it for yourself, it is bad interpretation that set sailed.

The fallen were just suppose to let humanity evolve on our own, because Life has been a test since the garden. Those secrets we were shown could have came in due time minus the evils that God mentioned for his overall judgment. Do not get the wrong idea about Enoch like some have. God loved him so much he did not let him die here on earth. The Archangel Uriel also showed

Enoch many secrets of the stars and planets before He was taken up to heaven for good. And, even some if not all of the fallen angels had good hearts. Make your own judgments, do not rely on others' opinions for they will surely defile you. Can we try to look at some people the same way too?

Many people confuse old school social code with actual Bible Code: not all rap music is gangster, cigarettes are unhealthy, but they're not a sin, cursing is not a sin, and fuck is only a bad word if used sexually. Anything that God made is not a sin, Jesus drank wine (Luke 7:34) but he refused it when it was spiked (Mark 15:23). However, moderation IS all over The Bible.

"For John the Baptist didn't drink wine and he often fasted, and you say, 'He's a demon possessed.' And I Son of Man, feast and drink, and you say, 'He's a glutton and a drunkard, and a friend of the worst sort of sinners.' But Wisdom is shown to be right by the lives of those who follow it!" (Luke 7:33-35)

I believe in reincarnation. It can explain why I never listened to anyone, have certain unexplained phobias, and experienced many Deja Vu's. This isn't my first go at life. Go ask Plato, Buddhists, Hindus, Essenes, and ALL the Mystics of the world about reincarnation. Jesus was an incarnate himself! Why couldn't we also be incarnated? You think Deja Vu is just some chemical reaction?! It is, but *Why does it react?! You have to think deeper! You're not going to The Root. Where there is Mystery; there is God. God has many names and there are many "Gods," but there is One True God. He is The Redeemer, He is ALL THINGS, He is The Universe. I ignored God, off and on, and came to those conclusions. I form my own opinions without bias. No one close to me does this. Now I do have a bias, I will always think God first, but that is not without 15 years of research off and on.

***Where There is Mystery; There is God

So, when I look around and I don't see Truth, I am pissed off. Now I am expressing it after bottling it up for so long! This past election did it for me and the following paragraph did it for me, but politics is all speculation and propaganda is all bullshit... A political leader can NEVER make everyone happy. The bickering back and forth is foolish. They're following the wrong rules. The rules were laid out for us, but we took it upon ourselves to elect kings. The two Books of Kings in the Old Testament is an illustration of what happens when God is not put first. This is self-explanatory. All would be well if we just followed The True Law. Israel Requests a King:

"Samuel was very upset with their request and went to The Lord for advice. 'Do as they say, but know that they are rejecting me, not you. They do not want me to be their king any longer, ever since I brought them out of Egypt they have forsaken me and followed other gods. And now they are giving you the same treatment. Do as they ask, but solemnly warn them about how a king will treat them" (1 Samuel 8:6-9).

Friends are no different. When you're apart of a group of friends, you're typically not allowed to be different than them and you end up following their lead at times (I was guilty of that). I am not saying I was an angel! I was also the ring leader, and I'm not saying I was a hardened criminal, but deep down I always knew how I was living was wrong and after the impulsive decisions I made, the next day I was always filled with guilt and I got so sick of feeling guilty. They say with sarcasm, "Why do you feel guilty?" No one puts themselves in another's shoes! They see it how they see it according to their lives! Don't listen to anyone! If you feel guilty then feel guilty. Your feelings are never wrong.

"Do Not Do What You Hate." Jesus Christ

I can't stress enough the importance of having the right role models and the right friends. Gradually, my snakeskin started to shed. I have fought on occasion with my friends over certain things and usually stood alone. It got to the point where we just couldn't get along anymore. I'm different and I love who I am now and it's because I walk alone that I can be Me. But, God Walks With Me.

Nothing is more "Gangsta" than being against the crowd. If peace for you means you have to leave your group of friends, do it. A True Rebel is for Peace. Jesus was a Gangsta, that is what most people do not understand. You do not get peace without some fighting. Non-violent fighting. Read the Gospels. They also had defense. "Peter put down that sword," said Jesus. How long did he have that sword for? It just shows up when Jesus got arrested? Jesus did not ask where it came from, but simply it is now time for me to make the sacrifice. Jesus talked some shit too He is the Son of God, you think the Son of God is just going to lay down and accept being mistreated? The only time He just sat back and took it was when He stood trial and had to carry the cross. People just tell followers of Jesus that they are not allowed to fight back. Not true whatsoever. Control your temper, but by no means are you to just sit back and let someone have their way with you. They just say this so they can get over on you. Read this,

"Do you think I have come to bring Peace to the Earth? No, I have come to bring Strife and Division!" Jesus (Luke 12:51)

"Do not imagine that I came to bring Peace to the Earth! No, I came with a Sword" (Matthew 10:34).

Your closest friends can be your worst enemies. We have all heard this. It can be very true, especially when you are changing and they are not. Some "friends" won't let you change and become who you want to be. You have to be like them in order to still hang out with them. A real friend lets you be who you want to be. You guys won't necessarily agree on anything anymore once the change begins to happen so it is best you both just go your separate ways. If you were apart of a trouble making group of friends, try to remember this... Boasting your "War Stories" only means you're embarrassed of your current righteousness... This will most likely lead you back to that bullshit.

When you are feeling like the outcast of the group, do not forget to stand your ground. It is your Truth and that is all that matters. Be your own person. And realize this, when your friends talk over whatever issue there is with the rest of your friends and they agree, does this make you wrong? Or does this make you right and them all wrong? Stand your ground. It is all opinions on their behalf. Just because majority rules does not mean anything! Typically, most people do not possess the ability to empathize.

That is the ability to put themselves in your shoes before forming an opinion. Most of the time they give us an opinion without us even asking for it. They just cannot grasp it, whatever it is, because it is not them, so only they see it as it is for them, not you. They only see it how they would see it according to their lives! You have to be above that. You are not an outcast! Don't listen to your friends, they are not you. Just cause it worked for them does not mean it can work you, they're just confusing you.

"Never cut your bodies in the mourning for the dead or mark your skin with tattoos, for I am the Lord." That is the one that did it for people to tell us no tattoos, but if this was really so why did God Himself tattoo Cain? Genesis 4:15, "If anyone kills Cain, Cain shall be avenged 7 times, so the Lord put a *mark* on him so he would not be killed on sight." (Leviticus 19:28)

The footnotes for Leviticus 19:28 say this, "Probably refers to the ancient practice of marking a slave with its owner's name and branding yourself with a devotion to a God." (Why was slavery permitted? Hold on I will get to that). Anyways, idol worship just kept popping up back then during the time of Moses. TWO of the Ten Commandments are about Idol worship! Remember the Golden Calf? I am sure there were others too, "Do not make idols out of birds or animals or fish." Why would He say that if it was not happening? You can tattoo those things on you, but don't worship them. We are not putting False Gods on our bodies right?

When Jesus came He undid a few laws Moses put in, but

He in no way was changing God's law, "Do not think I have come to abolish the laws of Moses and the Prophets, No, I came to fulfill them (Matthew 5:17). Jesus came to stand His ground, no compromises. What Jesus -also- did in chapter 5 of Matthew was Explain Further, because people had evolved, and also they were finding loopholes in the law, even the leaders of the temples were (Matthew 23). Now here is the evidence for the contradictions,

"Moses permitted divorce as a concession to your hard-hearted wickedness, but it was not what God had originally intended. And I tell you this, a man or woman who divorces and marries another commits adultery, unless someone has been unfaithful" (Matthew 19:8-9).

"And Jesus answered, 'Seek not the law in your scriptures, for the law is life, whereas the scripture is dead. I tell you truly, Moses received 10 Commandments from God, but the people felt they were too hard. Moses had compassion for his people and he said', 'Suffer, Lord, that I give them other laws since they are not with Thee, let them not be against Thee.' Jesus then said the law is, 'In the grass, in the tree, in the river, in the mountain, in the birds of heaven, in the fishes of the sea; but seek it chiefly in yourselves.'" (Essene Gospel of Peace)

The Essenes do not discount The Bible whatsoever, just understand the evolution of humanity. In man's law (religion and government) there will always be contradictions, but The Truth is all around and most importantly in ourselves. You just have to be sensitive enough to recognize it. This is why women are of the utmost importance in this world, they can bring sensitivity. Women are also the reason why Essene literature was not permitted in The Bible, because they empowered women.

There's a difference between The 10 Commandments and Moses' Laws. Moses' Laws that were not Prefaced by "The Lord" were Compromises or Details of a Commandant. The 10 Commandments IS God's Law and that is how God Originally Intended It To Be.

"Do not misunderstand why I have come. I did not come to abolish the law of Moses or the writings of the Prophets. No, I came to fulfill them. I assure you, until Heaven and Earth disappear, even the smallest detail of God's law will remain until its purpose is achieved. So if you break the smallest commandment and teach others to do the same, you will be the least in the Kingdom of Heaven." (Matthew 5:17-19)

Man compromises. Religion was government, still is to a degree, but it has lost its dominion in America. We have to protect the good hearted, the "victims" by compromising with the hard ones. The hard ones would completely ignore God thus becoming more evil. That is how you bring people together, isn't it? Have to find common ground. Cannot just up and change everything at the drop of a hat, no one would follow suit if that was the case. If they did follow suit, Moses wouldn't have had to make such compromises that you will find all throughout the Torah. God has to exist here somewhat, so we can eventually follow suit. Louis CK gets it, go watch his Abraham Lincoln sketch from *Saturday Night Live*,

"The one thing I'm really tired of is arguing with slave owners about slavery as if they're not just fucking assholes. 'I just like owning people.' 'Oh yeah I get that.' (Like you gotta act like you're totally cool with it) 'Yeah if I could own a couple of dudes I would own a couple of dudes, I just Kinda think that owning person is not cool... you stupid dick.'"

That is what Moses did when making the laws. He compromised with divorce, slavery, war, several others. That is the way people were, He compromised for them. Slavery time wasn't up yet. We did not evolve yet. That is clear in every history book since slavery has been around since *God knows when. *The Book of Enoch* explained one of the listed sins of the Fallen Angels was that they were suppose to evolve on our own right. Some fallen were trying to help us along, but they also did commit various evils as earlier explained. The world is a test, it has been a test since God planted the tree we weren't suppose to eat from, but yet we had to stare at it everyday. Why was it "Planted?"

Look where we are now. There are no slaves anymore. Every kind of race was enslaved at one point, whether by another race or by their neighbors, as a whole group/tribe or race or an individual, no matter what the color of your skin was. The problem currently is that African-Americans were the last to get it. Actually, second to last, the holocaust was the last act of slavery on earth and it was worse than any bout of slavery in all of history, but we are still feeling the aftershocks of those earthquakes, blacks more so than jews. How could God let all this happen? No, it is how could *man* let all this happen.

You have to realize that: Slaves, Homeless, Addicts, the Depressed, and so on are ***Blessed, If you keep the faith and follow the rules (Matthew 12:42-48). You do not get Heaven without Hell. (Matthew 5:5) from the Sermon on the Mount, Jesus said,

"BLESSED ARE THE MEEK FOR THEY SHALL INHERIT THE EARTH"

Meek means being Righteous while Suffering by following the gospels even during a hard life. You will be rewarded if you give when you need, but ONLY if you do not expect anything in return. Being completely unselfish like that, sometimes is easy and sometimes it is hard. We are selfish by nature. When I was first awakened, it was pure magic, I was completely selfless. I was "moved by every breath of wind." Then I calmed down some. God I miss being that in tune, but it always comes back when you live righteously. Jesus said to, "Go the extra mile when asked." (Matthew 5:41-42)

Back to laws made according to the times. God also said in (Leviticus 19:27), "Do not cut off the hair on your temples or clip the edges of your beard." What were they doing back then that made this a sin? You know damn well that cutting your hair and trimming your beard is Not a Sin. Why? Remember what Paul said in Romans 1:19, "For The Truth about God is known to us intuitively in our hearts." It was a law made for the time. How can I be so sure? Well because it wasn't "Set in Stone" and pun is so intended right there! It would have been on the Ten Commandments if it was suppose to last. You know in your hearts which ones are a keeper and which ones are not. So

Leviticus 19:28 was not set in stone! This is The Truth right here from Mark chapter 7, and I am summarizing,
"It is not what goes into your body that defiles you! It is the Thought-Life that defiles you! If it does not come into contact with your heart, it does not defile you!"

Your actions and your thoughts defile you, nothing else. Sex can defile you, but Christ is a lot more liberal than people have led you to believe. Sex before marriage is NOT a sin, adultery and sexual immorality is. Meaning you can make love without being married, but it has to be love! All Jesus said was, "Do not commit adultery and do not lust, even if you lust in your mind" (Matthew 5:27-28).

Obviously this makes pornography a sin. If you think it is OK then you obviously have lied to yourself too much for your own selfish pleasure. It is a clear violation of the law. Watching porn and being in porn is still the same sin, just on different levels. You know damn well that it is no good for you. Of course I speak from experience. I was a "guy" once, but I do not know what I am anymore. I do not know anyone else like me. I can imagine what it is like to be gay because I know how it feels to be an outcast because of simply who I am.

Jesus said when asked about *divorce, "They record that from the beginning, 'God made Them male and female.' This explains why a man leaves his father and mother and is joined to his wife, and the two become one. Since they are no longer two but one, let no one separate them, for God has joined them together." (Matthew 19:4-6)

This is the closest saying of Christ we have to compare to whether or not homosexuality is allowed. I don't think God knows how this happened, but no one should ever be alienated. The Golden rule applies to everyone. Is it possible that God has learned to accept it? I do not want to say it because I do not want to break any hearts, but we were not made for the same sex, that is the truth. All throughout the Old Testament, it is a big no no. At first it started out as a complete sin, it was barbaric or lustful. Have you ever heard about how Old men would lust after their young apprentices? The Greeks are famous for this. I am not going to cite those sources in the Old Testament, you are well aware of them if you are gay. This gives no one the right to condemn you though. The Golden Rule applies to everyone! Why didn't Jesus mention homosexuality, while Moses did many times? In Matthew 19:8-9, "That is not what God had originally intended." Jesus explained how Moses had to compromise with the people for the placement of a law. Why wouldn't there be a compromise here if it is based in love?

Now this is all speculation, but I am using the God inside me that Paul said we all have in Romans 1:19 with the above scripture in Matthew 19:8-9 plus seeing that Jesus did not mention homosexuality obviously like Moses and Jesus covers ALL grounds... How could God punish you for something you have no control over? If you are truly only attracted to the same sex then how could He punish you. It was not a choice right? Did an ex cause this rebellion in you? Did friends manipulate you into believing you're something you're not? Even if you did do that out of choice: sorry do not get startled, wait until after the quote to have an emotion for this applies to all (Luke 12:48),

"But for people who are not aware that they are doing wrong will be punished only lightly. Much is required from to whom much is given, and much more is required from those to whom much more is given."

Now what would a light punishment be from God? Probably not too bad, depending on what it was you did and whether or not you repented. If you are gay, do you feel like you are doing wrong? I have no say on this, we were not made for the same sex, but if you really cannot control yourself then it is obviously a sexual orientation that evolved on its own. God left us here to evolve on our own, anything could happen, and I don't think He knows how that happened.

Is homosexuality a sin? I don't think it is anymore, but it is not my call. I say, IF you're not running around acting like sluts you should be fine. Same rules apply to you too. "Do not lust, even with your mind" and "No Sexual Immorality." I think that was always the biggest problem, the fact that it could not be out in the open and because it became so secret, only lust could come to the surface. When you desire something you can't have so hard, then only those evils inside you will come out. This is why Buddha taught to remove all desire to avoid suffering. God feels for you! He hates to see his people suffer. When you have a true heart He will protect you! Remember, "If it does not come into contact with your heart, it does not defile you." Jesus also said, "And when you make the male and the female one in the same, so that the male not be male nor the female the female, then you will enter the kingdom." Meaning just do not exist, you just are. Just like God is. God is Male and Female in One (Genesis 1:27). This also applies to transgender obviously. It is not what is on the outside that is a sin, it is your inside! Your body does not matter, it is your spirit that matters. Once again, "If it does not come into contact with your heart, it does not defile you and No Sexual Immorality."

I am not messing with abortion, not gonna do it. Nope. It is hard, but I have to. It is not the way that *God Had Originally Intended It*," we all know this. Now, this is for men also, not just women. God doesn't judge your actions as much as He judges WHY you did it. He knows your heart and your thoughts. God also understands product of environment (I've proven this already) and also "Knowing not what we do." IT IS THE MAN's FAULT. He is the one that gets to be the scapegoat. He plants the seed and gets to wait for a decision from her, he thinks he can walk away clean, nope. It is his fault.

The children's generations could benefit from the outlawing of abortion because obviously people need punishments hanging over their head to not do something they shouldn't do. Have we not gotten more sexual and vain overall on this planet? Is putting a law on abortion our last hope? We should not need laws in the first place. We shouldn't have needed a Bible at all, but people's actions made it that way. We have became so careless with sex that what else can we do for our children?

There are so many variables to deem whether an abortion is right or not, but whether or not it is a sin is up to God. New laws are brought into this world when things start getting out of hand. Have we reached our limit? Putting a ban on abortion could make our children RESPECT sex more. We typically do not listen to our parents and some do not even have the right parents to teach them right from wrong, so a ban on abortion could help us as a whole have more pure relationships... the way it is supposed to be. It shouldn't have to be this way, but people who always lean towards selfish thinking need to know there is a consequence: 9 times out of 10 it is the man's fault because we are the ones who typically start this. Men plant the seed. Then the decision gets placed on women and the man is forgotten about. Sound familiar? It is Adam and Eve all over again. Once this happens, the woman goes into a panic, and because of the accepted moral code of society, abortion is always an option during this panic. Remember, adoption is always an option too!

So, why are we fighting to keep adoption when no one wants to do it! I understand the 'just in case' factor, but why not take it a step back further and just have sex with the right one or if you must have sex, wrap it up and pull out. I have proven Biblically how much we can actually be free here on earth and still be Godly, but there is no excuse for abortion except maybe the obvious case of sexual assault. That is God's decision though. So wrap it up and pull out even when the woman is on birth control, or like I said make sure the person is the right person.

Realize, could this man or woman be a good parent, before committing to sex. And, Be In Love! Sex is supposed to be about love and love only, nothing else. Sure inside relationships you may not always feel that love, but because the relationship is based on love then it is just fine. Sex is like anything though, moderation is the key to getting the most enjoyment out of it. This is much harder for young people. Sometimes sex is had just because, and its not even lust. At least with lust there is some kind of emotion and passion depending on what you are actually thinking. Do not confuse attraction with lust. You know the difference. One is animalistic and the other is more genuine.

Men should be loaded with hormones in their 30s when we have matured, not when we are in our teens and twenties and complete morons. Men most likely wouldn't have put these women in those circumstances! We are typically the aggressors during sex so it is up to us to be more careful. It is just as much as our faults as it is the woman's, if not more... The man may have told her that he did not want the abortion, but did he mean it? God knows where your heart is. Just because he said it, does not mean that he meant it. If the guy says, "Well she wanted the abortion, not me." Usually that comment is obviously a tell tale sign that he is lying depending on how he said it. God knows where your heart is, you might have fooled your family and friends dude, but not God. Remember Adam's sin in the Garden, besides eating the fruit too, was that he just sat back and watched Eve sin and then he snitched on her right away when God questioned him. Eve got fooled by the serpent just as much as she may have been fooled by friends and family around her pushing her towards abortion. That girl who ended up going through with the abortion, may not be at fault at all. It is not what you do, it is why you do it.

I am sorry you had to hear this, but I know that some of you deal with it deep down, and I wanted to show you that God is more fair than you think because of what the outspoken people of the world about abortion have said. Who are they to condemn you? They are nobody. I am sure they have hurt you. They are wrong. Does not mean you can do it; you're forgiven for being a product of environment if you repent. No one is exempt from repentance. To repent, one must not tell anyone and be genuine about it. Feel the guilt and act on it.

We do not need more people acting like many men. Yes I am talking to you, my lesbian friends. Here is one that many, mostly men, have to hear "Just go get laid." Like this fixes problems; it usually makes more. If not for him, then for her. This is a clear violation of Jesus saying "Do not lust, even with your mind." Sex is supposed to be sacred! It is suppose to be love making, not fucking. Maybe we could just start by calling it a better name instead of fucking, banging, etc. Just call it sex, love, etc. If we call it a better name we could think better of it, no? Of course I am guilty of just having sex just to have it. I grew up though. Even in my 30s it is considered weird to not just want to have meaningless sex. Friends will swear up and down that I am crazy. I stay true to myself. I have had enough of that bullshit.

Ignorant opinions are typically rooted in an inability to empathize, other than being uninformed, and sometimes being informed does not help them think more fairly. How many times a day do you hear people just talking out of their ass? Has to be several. How many times does high confidence win the wrong arguments? It's time for humble people to start being louder. "If you are judged then judge in the same measure.

"How can one worry about a speck in one person's eye when you have a log in your own. First take care of the log in your own eye; then perhaps you will see well enough to deal with the speck in your friend's eye" (Matthew 7:4-5)

Then you have more general arguments and even on higher levels this happens. Why do these arguments even happen when we all have smartphones? The Paradigm Shift of the Smartphone is here for a reason, and I don't want to hear that you're busy, it takes 2 minutes to look anything up... anything! Stop taking things at face value. Do not be like the ignorant. Knowledge is power, it is true. Even when you have done the research and prove some wrong, they will still hold on to their opinion. They want everything to go their way:

"How shall I describe this generation? We played weddings songs and you weren't happy, so we played funeral songs, but you weren't sad" (Luke 7:31-32)

Denial Is Ignorance; Humility Will Set You Free.

Knowing history sheds ignorance, which brings understanding, and understanding fills us with Love. We all know how to Love those close to us, but ignorance keeps us from the others. There's actually a reasonable explanation for all the misconceptions in some people's hearts, but many just don't want to hear it. By refusing to hear the truth you're refusing Love. Can you tell I have been surrounded by Ignorance most of my life? None of this is directed towards you, unless it applies. Sorry, but we as people cannot be talking out of our ass anymore. All the knowledge of the world is at our fingertips, there is no excuse to be ignorant. Some people say some ignorant shit, but they do mean well. The double standard is a good example. Like when complaining about affirmative action if a white man is more qualified for the job, but then the black man gets the job because the job needed someone from the minority so they would not be in trouble with the authorities. This person has every right to complain, but is it fair for the black man who, historically, has had a very hard time finding a job, any job. That black man can, in time, become just as qualified as the other person was. It is all about opportunities, that the minorities are still having problems with today. If two white guys go for the same job and one has an uncle in management and the other doesn't, who is more likely to get the job? For a black guy, everyone he is up against has an uncle in management. People just do not know how to empathize. It does not mean this person is necessarily racist for not empathizing. Yes, some use it as a mask for their "inner racist" but others are just emotionally guarded... I'm sure we all can understand that. Some are definitely racist when you hear ignorance like that, but it's up to you to dig deeper into that person to see where they're at. Don't let a first impression deter you from finding the truth. Here is a first-hand example.

This one is so tragic to me. I forget his name but I'm going to call him, Shock, cause even I was scared of him as he was approaching as I was talking to this homeless girl standing in the corner near the exit to the street. I was asking if she had a place to go and she could barely answer, so I asked if there were any other girls out here that she could stick with. I kept insisting she had to find girls to stick with. I felt someone coming because in Union Station in Denver it's like a general population for the homeless and I decided to mingle with all of them as I waited for my train at 3:15 am and I got there couple hours early because it was a Monday and I was tired.

In strolls this black man, black hood, baggy pants, and the walk with it. I thought this was the little white girls pimp so I started walking away, but he kept walking past the girl so I said what's up. When this happens it all happens so fast, but man, dude was upset, and here is the kicker! He's upset because he has been giving his ex-girlfriend money and she's been sleeping with another man. He says he can't stop giving her money. I start flipping out! Hard. He lost a grand last week to her and he's been homeless. I'm flipping out on him now like any hot headed Italian would. He has pretty steady income but he is giving it to his ex! And he calls her his girl still?! I thought he was a pimp! I asked if he had a record, he did, I didn't ask why, but he had a job. He would get picked up for simple labor help. Same went with the white dude with red hair from the south that had Italian blood in him. Just do the simple labor jobs. He was sitting alone near the actual train tracks. It was his first night there so I told him to mingle with the others, but he just wanted to be alone. He actually prefers it. He doesn't really, but he loves not having responsibilities. He told me his family life and where he was from but I forget it, I talked to so many people I always have so much going on in my head all the time and it was 2:30 in the morning. But here's the kicker, I thought Shock was a pimp.

Here's a man who is so desperate for any kind of love he puts himself on the street. I just tell him to save his money, don't give her shit, and then he started to repeat that out loud. I think he might stick to it, I don't know. I thought he was a fucking pimp. I am still in Shock. He is the complete opposite of a pimp. The young girl in the corner better find some girls to run with or a decent man, because there are decent men out there on the streets. They are all rebels to society and they stick together. This election makes me think they are right, but everyone has that one piece of inner light that needs to be focused on to fix the rest of you, that light is your purpose.

Everyone judges books by the cover in this world. The benefit of the doubt does not even exist. I showed the same behavior, but you still have to keep it real. Stereotypes exist for a reason, sometimes the shoe fits. Still have to be careful. I gave them all a chance and I was proven wrong! It was great to be proven wrong in this way, there is hope for people. There is always those few bad apples that ruin it for the bunch. I just know I was suppose to write about these stories.

Last three times I flew on a plane, I was next to a rabbi or former rabbi. First couple times I paid it no mind, this last time I did though. It was the flight out to Phoenix. I was writing in my notebook and the former rabbi next to me was reading a book on how to write. He wanted to write a book on all the people he helped and I was just writing song lyrics. I did not pay this any mind at the time until I returned home after Denver and I realized... *Ok last three flights out west I sat by a rabbi. Nothing happened with the first two. This last one wanted to write about his stories of helping people, but couldn't, and I ended up helping people, something I never did before like this, and I can already write. Ok God, thanks for showing me the signs, I will get right on it* ... That is synchronicity.

Where does ignorance start? With bad apples and gossip. Many words out of peoples' mouths is gossip when pertaining to others. Of course this applies to politics and religion too. People ruin everything. Anything that sounds like gossip you have to stay away from. I can't stress this enough, don't be that bored, and don't look for reasons to promote your agenda, because you're sure to find it. Wait for the truth to emerge before you make a fuss, I know it's hard to determine what's the truth or what isn't because politicians, the media, and people we know have ruined that for us but you should be able to figure it out. Our friends and acquaintances have made this even harder for us. How much does a person gossip from day to day? My God. People have nothing better to do than to talk about others all the while ignoring themselves. Putting down others for their "faults." I have done this, I am not exempt, but just because you sinned yesterday does not mean you cannot run with it today! Just stop doing it and you are forgiven.

"What sorrows await you who laugh carelessly, for your laughing will turn to mourning and sorrow" (Luke 6:25)

"Obscene stories, foolish talk, and crude jokes—these are not for you. Instead let their be thankfulness to God" (Ephesians 5:4)

"Then Peter asked Jesus, 'Explain what you meant when you said people aren't defiled by what they eat.'

"Don't you understand?" Jesus asked him. "Anything you eat passes through your stomach and then goes out your body. But evil words come from an evil heart and defile the person who says them. For for the heart comes evil thoughts, murder, adultery, all other sexual immorality, theft, lying, and slander. There are what defile you. Eating with unwashed hands could never defile you and make you unacceptable to God!" (Matthew 15:15-20)

How does righteousness prevail if we remain humble in the face of "those people." You can be humble all while being arrogant about it. It is possible! It is not what you say, it is how you say it. The right people will recognize The Truth. You'll know when you hear The Truth cause the moral will always be Fair. That's why Jesus had to die, people couldn't believe because they were too ignorant to comprehend what is fair. Because God built us to Love and when you don't recognize HIS perfect creation when he shows you it, He is ashamed of how low your spirit grade is. Jesus had to die because that was the times they were in, that's what it called for, people were more barbaric back then. That's the only way to prove a point. There were many martyrs back then: God never chose just Jesus. Why would all the religions believe so hard in something if it wasn't their own truth. So we were left to think about it, in guilt... Majority of people still don't get it. How do I know this? I just do and so do you. I promise to you that I wrote these last two paragraphs before I came across this point-

"God shows his anger from Heaven against all sinful people that push the Truth away from themselves, For the truth about God is known to them Instinctively. God has put this knowledge in their hearts."
Romans 1:19-20

Jesus Christ had to die, other than for our sins, but because too many people were guilty for not believing in him, we pushed away The Truth. His Good News still had to be brought to the four corners of the world for us to be saved and we stopped this from happening... Or Did IT Happen?

***HINDU, HARE KRISHNA (The Energy of Christ)

"When a person responds to the joys and sorrows of others as if they were their own, he has attained the highest state of spiritual union"
Krishna

Hindu comes from the Sanskrit word Sindhu, which is from the Indus River in Northwest India, where Pakistan and North India is now. You don't get Buddha without Hindu. Buddha's teaching is just like Jesus. Love and compassion, it is so simple. Buddhism is a branch of Hindu, not a Root. Hindu is a true Spiritual practice. There is no "Vatican," no leaders (Remember, I love Pope Francis). This is Not a Religion. This is Sanatana Dharma "The Eternal Law" is "A Way of Life."

The Vedas are their first words, their Roots. The Vedas first arrived around 1500 BC, plus or minus a few hundred years, around the same time as the Sumerian Tablets, which is where we got the roots of The Bible from. Coincidence? Ancient sages received this scripture from the "Essence." Brahma is a part of their "Trinity" with Vishnu and Shiva. Krishna is the Avatar of Lord Vishnu. The Hindu Creation History has NO Concept of Original Sin. Choice/Karma is just Innate, Born with It.

The creation history in Hindu from *The Vedas* leads me to believe that The Devil is separate from The Serpent. You know the serpent from Genesis right? The entity that tricked Adam and Eve into eating from the tree of knowledge. Before time on earth began, the serpent was floating on the waters with Lord Vishnu asleep in its coils, keeping Him safe. Then sound began, OHM. Ohmmm. Lord Vishnu woke up and arose a lotus flower from His navel, and in the flower was Brahma. Vishnu gave Brahma the job to create a world here on this water. Remember how I talked about the Two Gods from The Bible, from the words of Jesus Christ (God of the Living and God of the Dead). Brahma split Himself into Two, creating both Male and Female, sound familiar again too right? Brahma split into two for man and woman.

Now, we all know what Yoga and Karma is, but how about Nirvana? This is the ultimate goal, to be in complete union with God. Perfect unselfishness and self-awareness! If you cannot reach Nirvana here on Earth, then you're going to have to keep coming back to Earth until you get it right. This is Samsara, the cycle of: birth, life, death, and rebirth. Plato will attest to this and every Mystic on Earth... including some Christians. Reincarnation is a Gift and a Curse. Gift to fix it and a curse because we have to.

"It is harder for a camel to pass through the eye of a needle than for someone to enter the Kingdom of Heaven" (Matthew 19:24).

Haven't you ever heard of Jesus Christ, very possibly, spending time in Kashmir during those lost 18 years of his teens and young adulthood. Kashmir has Hindu and Islamic Roots. They even have a name for Him, Issa, and in Islam Jesus is known as Isa and respected as a prophet and the messiah. Jesus could have very possibly been respected as The Son of God in Islam, but since we have fought with each other forever, they could not respect that. But, we don't even give respect to Muhammad at all! And, it was the Angel Gabriel that came to Muhammad! Who is wrong here?

Jesus could have also been here with The Native

Americans and in Britain. If you believe He is Son of God, couldn't He do anything His Father wanted him to do? Jesus was not just a man, He was also Spirit, right? If Krishna is the reincarnation of Lord Vishnu then Jesus could be the reincarnation of The Holy Spirit right? The God of the Dead.

Speaking of Christ, Krishna could have been Jesus! Christ comes from the word Krista. Krista is Krishna. Krishna is Krista. Christ means *The Anointed One*. It's just different languages and their teachings are the same. It's just catered to different cultures. There was no internet back then, the Son of God had to spread the necessary Good News by foot. Christ had to travel to the four corners of the world right? If Jesus was/is the Son of God, could he not reincarnate into any body He chooses? How strong is your faith in Jesus? Krishna said,

"I Am the Beginning, Middle, and End of Creation"

Go get yourself *The Bhagavad Gita* and read all about Krishna! Krishna came about 1000 years earlier than Jesus. Both were born by a virgin surrounded by angels and wise men bearing gifts. Both births caused the kings to issue the murder of all infants in the town to prevent the prophesy from coming true. What prophesy? Both were born for our salvation, that prophesy. Krishna was called the "Sin bearer" "The Redeemer" and also "Jezeus" which means "Pure Essence" (That one is just too similar, Jezues). Both used parables to teach, lived poor and loved the poor. Healed the sick and raised the dead. Krishna is also supposed to come back and do battle with evil. You know what, I don't even want to explain further, or was that enough? I could be wrong here of course that Jesus is Krishna, but if I am wrong, the Spirit was still True in Krishna and that is all that should matter. No one can prove this. I believe it is possible considering the similarities in the history. Either way, Jesus most likely spent some time in India during those lost years of his teens and twenties or His Spirit was in Lord Krishna's. Either way, it does not matter which God or Savior you believe in, as long as you believe and your heart is true! We all have the same God anyways. The Holy Spirit is within every religion. There is an all encompassing essence of love that can be felt with belief and concentration.

Meditation just like Buddhism itself is rooted from the Hindus. Buddhism somewhat is for a person with a spiritual self, but cannot imagine there being a "God." In Buddhism there is no creator of the world. It is a spiritual philosophy, that says we are like Gods, just as I mentioned earlier Jesus saying, "Is it not written in your law that you are gods." They are mystics and I can get down with a mystic any day. We know the story in the Garden where once we ate from the Tree of Knowledge we became like Gods knowing all about good and evil. During my twenties, it was easier for me to understand the Buddhist practices because I did not understand the true story of the Garden of Eden yet. I never realized that God planted the tree and never asked myself why even plant it in the first place? It was the evil in the world that led me to other spiritual paths. I did not realize it just the fault of choice.

A famous man named Alan Watts helped me along this spiritual path. You can find his lectures all over YouTube and there's books to read too. He brought Buddhism, the Tao, and other religions and philosophies from the East out into the public eye of America, but he was from England. He was a counterculture figure in the 1960s, but he was highly educated, he was not a hippie. He spoke about all the Eastern Religion's and Philosophies. He said, "Buddhism can be thought of as a form of psychotherapy, not a religion," in his book *Psychotherapy East and West*. I highly suggest Alan Watts for a starting point to the Eastern Religions and Philosophies as well as Consciousness. Consciousness is a great starting point to any spiritual endeavor. I do not mean to offend anyone, but in all of Buddha's righteousness there is a vanity to it because they acknowledge no creator and I am well aware of Job 38, 39, 40, 41, and 42:

""Where were you when I laid the foundations of Earth, Who marked off its dimensions... Surely you know! Can you bind the chains of the Pleiades, Can you loosen the belt of Orion?"

"There are no distinct texts on the actual words of the Buddha claiming to be from the Buddha himself, just like Jesus, so oral tradition begot texts of his life and teachings by his followers. Buddha started his life in luxury. Married the princess Yashodhara who would be the mother of his son, but at age 29 he would come to leave them for a devotion to spirituality. He was sheltered his whole life, kept away from the sight of the real world and when he finally went out on a chariot ride outside the palace he saw all the suffering of the real world, and that is when he decided he should give everything up and live the life the of an ascetic. Ascetics are deep mystics. They fast, meditate everyday, live in poverty, no luxuries whatsoever. They were most likely of the spiritual sect called "Jains." Like Buddhism they were somewhat atheists and made the practice more personal, but understood we had a soul and there was an essence out there in the universe. After 6 years of this extreme practice he grew so weak he fainted in a river and realized this was not for him. Then he sat under a tree, meditated and meditated, and received The Four Noble Truths: Suffering, Origin of Suffering, Removing Desire, Liberation of Suffering. Then the preaching began. (*Buddhism*)"

Everyone suffers. We all go through different types of suffering. We are all built differently so suffering really is all relative. A person watching the Miami Dolphins lose in the playoffs again and again could have the same exact feeling of suffering as someone that just got sentenced to 30 days in jail. Sounds crazy, but it is true. I am sure you can think of many examples yourself. We all know the saying, "God only gives us what we can handle." Happiness comes in bits and pieces, moments of decency, success, and love. Not everyone is exempt from happiness, no one is exempt from suffering, and no one is exempt from the Word.

The Church of Jesus Christ the Latter-Day Saints, you know them as Mormons. The story goes that in the 4th century a prophet named Mormon was given sacred records to write down from God and later his son Moroni would finish it and bury them in a hill in upstate west New York. Fast forward 1,400 years and Moroni appeared as an angel to Joseph Smith and told him about the buried records and thus began the process of transcribing them.

Anything is possible with God. Jesus Christ is their savior, so what laws are they breaking? Polygamy right. Well they actually stopped the practice of polygamy around 1890. Yes, some still practiced it, but they were not under the jurisdiction of the church itself, they were heretics. Few bad apples always ruin the bunch. Are their origins hard to believe? Sure. God just wants us to believe and it is possible that God did arrange this to baptize more believers in the heart of America. It was a success and Joseph Smith was martyred in doing so. (*Mormonwiki*)

They did not just make up the practice of polygamy. Yes, we were originally intended to have just one spouse, that is right in Genesis 2:24, "This explains why a man leaves his father and mother and is joined to his wife and the two become one." Deuteronomy 17:17 says that, "A king should not have multiple wives because it takes the attention away from God." King Solomon had Many wives (1 Kings 11) and that chapter shows how it affected his relationship with God. Solomon would not even obey God's command to not worship other Gods. Genesis 4:19 has Lamech being the first to be married to two women. Why was this allowed? It does not say so this is open for speculation. Is it possible that this was to multiply the earth with more of God's chosen genetics? To keep more women from harm in the streets? Or is it male shamanistic? That is up to you to play with, but we can't come to a conclusion because we don't know the truth. More accounts of polygamy are with Moses, David, and Jacob. Those are some heavy hitters in the Old Testament. Jesus said to not commit adultery, but is it adultery if the other woman is also your wife? We should not be trying to find loopholes! No. Jesus is all about the original plan of God like I have mentioned before in His teaching on divorce where He quotes Genesis 2:24. How could Two become One if there are Three or Four? Cannot happen. We know in our hearts that it is wrong. That is all you need in life; trust your heart. Do unto others.

"I have other sheep too, that are not in this sheepfold. I must bring them also, and they will listen to my voice; and there will be one flock with one shepherd." (John 10:16)

Jesus has sheep everywhere. He had to cover the four corners of the world right? Of course, this is a tough one to speak about since the Natives of the Americas did not have, for the most part, written language way back when, like there was in the east, and what was written/drawn still has not been completely deciphered; it is all oral tradition. Except the Mayans have something called the *Popol Vuh*, which was brought to us by way of a Dominican Priest named Francisco Ximenez during the 18th century for the translation. Just because it is oral tradition does it make it false? My Mother's Sunday gravy was passed down from my Grandma and from hers. Their might have been minor changes in the seasoning or the meatballs, but it is still the truth. Only Jesus is more truthful than my Mother's gravy.

The creation stories between each tribe of the Americas and the *Popol Vuh* all differ in detail, but the one commonality is that there is an essence that controls the forces of the universe, "The Great Spirit." Also a world that had to be done over a few times, before we came about. The Flood is also mentioned. The Aztecs mention our earth having to be done over a few times by global catastrophes. I believe in Atlantis, we know about the dinosaurs, the ice age, and Noah. In Maya they have "The Hero Twins" and Hunab Ku was the creator of the universe and Itzamna was the son of Ku. The Aztecs have Two Gods as well: Ometecuhtli, "The Lord of Duality," and Omeciuatl, "The Lady of Duality," and the Incas have Viracocha who made the earth and all living things: knowing about the Universal Spirit? Like Israel and Christians. These all sound a lot like the Hindu tradition and The Bible too, remember the God of the living and the God of the dead? And, Lord Shiva can be called duality. Why? Because it is said Shiva has no father.

We know about the human sacrifices. I will spare you the details, but they just did not know what they were doing yet. They thought they were pleasing the Gods by returning souls to them, until a God by the name of Quetzalcoatl by the Aztecs and known as Kukucaln by the Maya, came around and said human sacrifice was wrong! Also wanted to be the savior of the world. The name Quetzalcoatl means "Feathered Serpent." Do not get confused about the serpent, remember The Serpent and Vishnu? The Serpent birthed Vishnu. Feathers represent our spiritual origins and the serpent represents reality. Quetzalcoatl had a twin named Xololtl, thus giving us two serpents. Ever look at the modern logo for medicine? Why does the symbol of medicine have two snakes wrapped around an angelic wing topped pole? Almost looking like a cross with wings wrapped in two snakes, or even the DNA double helix. There are lots of theories to this: Aliens, Lucifer and Jesus, Greek God Hermes, even way back to the ancient Sumerians, but I am going with The Bible's of course, even though The Sumerians pre-date Moses: "Then the Lord told him, 'Make a replica of a poisonous snake and attach it to the top of the pole. Those who are bitten will live if they simply look at it!" (Numbers 21:8)

First time the "Feathered Serpent" was being worshipped was around 500 BC in the city of Teotihuacan, or even 1000 years earlier in the Olmec culture. You can find ancient pyramids in Teotihuacan known as "Where the Gods are from." He was initiated into the spiritual life through the sacred mushroom. He was also associated, like Jesus, with The Morning Star, the planet Venus. Quetzalcoatl had a twin named Xololtl and he was The Dawn Star, also planet Venus. He was the God of the underworld. Both virgin births. For these reasons -some- mormons believe them to be Jesus and Lucifer, because many of them believe them to be brothers. Remember all the angels are known as Sons and Daughters of God. Although there is a familiarity, the legends of these twins are not similar like Krishna was to Jesus. You'll have to do your own research, there is a lot to take in. I am here to keep it simple, just like the root, because that is all that is necessary.

It is said that it was believed the arrival of my Spaniards with Cortes was the reincarnation of Quetzalcoatl or the Prophesy fulfilled by Quetzalcoatl or the one they called "The Pale Master." Perhaps it wasn't as brutal as believed?

(More information can be found in *Quetzalcoatl* the References) or the book *The Gospel of the Toltecs* by Frank Diaz.

Going through every tribe in the Americas is like going through every denomination in the Christian religion. One thing we know for sure, that was a common thread between all the tribes of the Americas was humility! There was a Chief, but he was the most humble. He was no King, he was wisdom, he was a spiritual leader. Our Natives were connected to The Truth, the essence. We know the sacred mushroom helps propel us into that essence and the Shamans use this practice up until today. Perhaps something else also helped them along the way? Known by many names...

"The Healer spoke, 'As I watched you, I found you sinful in cunning warfare; I leave you peaceful and contented. I found you in slavery, I leave you free. Why have I talked to all tribes in their language? There are wild tribes in the jungle and they know not The Great Spirit of All."

"It is said the hot springs of Tacobya mark the passage of the Healer. In the canyons nearby Coso, where so lightly sleeps the Fire God and near it is the hand with the T cross, and next to it is Great Cross. The flame of the dawn touched his golden sandals, then with the whole tribe watching, they say to Him, "Stop and tap a large rock in the midst of the desert dryness with his long staff and behold there gushed water, now called The Spring of Tacobya." Just as Moses did, "I will be standing there in front of you in front of you in the rock of Horeb, strike the rock and water will flow from it for the people to drink" (Exodus 17:6).

*Known as The Pale One; The Pale Prophet. And, the Spaniards were also called "The White Man" as well as it was possibly prophesied by Quetzalcoatl, as said earlier.

"Once in the days long-vanished, with three great -ships- which had sailed from the Sunset-lands, came white-robed Wakea, the Fair God who healed the injured, raised the dead, and walked on water. He came to an outlying island of the Tahitian group where two tribes were fighting bitterly."

The book *He Walked the Americas* by L. Taylor Hansen will give you, in detail, all the Legends of our Natives by way of Christ, and there are many legends. You might ask yourself, ships? Jesus on a ship?

"Could you meet me in the country, in the summertime of England, could you meet me?" Van Morrison

There is also an old legend that Jesus visited England in the area which is in Glastonbury called Avalon; this is where the first Christian Church was built above ground. This was during Jesus' teenage years in which He was brought there by way of his rich uncle, Joseph of Arimathea who was a tin trader for the Roman empire and also the future Apostle of England starting in 37 AD. His Uncle Joseph is said to have been the guardian of Jesus after the death of his humanly father, Joseph, which happened sometime during Jesus' teens or twenties because there is no account of his death anywhere, or of him during the 3 years of Jesus's preaching. The last we heard of Joseph is when he and his wife Mary could not find Jesus, and they finally found him in the temple when he was 12 years old. (Luke 2:47-50)

So Uncle Joseph being a "guardian" would make sense considering, "Joseph was a secret disciple of Jesus (because he feared the Jewish leaders), and asked Pilate for permission to take Jesus's body down from the cross (John 19:38)." A family member would carry the casket right? He probably feared the leaders because he didn't want to lose his job... For more, read: *The Traditions of Glastonbury* by E. Raymond Capt and *Did Our Lord Visit Britain* by C.C. Dobson.

Now, since John the Baptist was Jesus' cousin, why didn't He recognize Him right away? How he did recognize Him (I believe) is because of His Spirit... Which is like The Prophet Elijah's as spoken by Jesus. "And if you believe it, he is Elijah, the one who said the prophets said would come" (Matthew 11:14). Elijah took on the 450 prophets of Baal alone and won with God beside him (1 Kings 18). A spirit that strong knows some things intuitively.

The Prophet Malachi, Jesus Christ, and the Angel Gabriel said:

Malachi on the prophesy of the Messiah: "Look, I am sending you the prophet Elijah before the great and dreadful day of the Lord arrives." (Malachi 4:5)

Jesus said about John: "If you are willing to accept what I say, he is Elijah, the one the prophets said would come." (Matthew 11:14)

Gabriel said to John's parents: "He will be a man with the spirit and power of Elijah, the prophet of old. He will precede the coming of the Lord, preparing the people for His arrival." (Luke 1:17)

Since John did not recognize Him right away, can lead us to believe that Jesus was not living in Judea during those years between the ages of 12-30. Remember, they were cousins. Or, at least Jesus was just not around that much. I am sure He was busy, learning to be God. John the Baptist was probably pretty busy too. People of the town still recognized Jesus though, "Is this not Joseph's son" (Luke 4:22). I would think it would be very hard to recognize someone comparing before and after puberty, 17 years after puberty no less. Was He recognized right away or were there whispers to find out if it was the boy Jesus?

C.C. Dobson wrote, "As a boy, He was brought merely for a visit by Joseph of Arimathea on one of his voyages. Later as a young man He returned and settled at Glastonbury for the purpose of quiet study, prayer, and meditation. Here He erected for Himself a small house of mud and wattles."

And in one of my favorite songs by Van Morrison "*Summertime in England,*" he sings, "Did you ever hear about Jesus walkin,' down by Avalon." Van also mentions T.S. Eliot and William Blake. Blake wrote a short poem in the preface to his epic
"Prelude to Milton"

And did those feet in ancient time
Walk upon England's mountains green?
And was the holy Lamb of God
On England's pleasant pastures seen?

And did the Countenance Divine
Shine forth upon our clouded hills?
And was Jerusalem builded here
Among these dark Satanic Mills?
Bring me my Bow of burning gold:
Bring me my Arrows of desire:
Bring me my Spear: O Clouds unfold!
Bring me my Chariot of fire.
I will not cease from Mental fight,
Nor shall my sword sleep in my hand
Till we have built Jerusalem
In England's green and pleasant land.

He may have been in England, but Jesus was still darker than an Italian in August. Jesus is from the Tribe of Judah from the bloodline of David, the largest Tribe of Israel. One can confirm this by going to Matthew 1 or Luke 3 in your Bible. The Tribe of Judah among the other tribes of Israel started scattering throughout the earth, this was called the Jewish Diaspora,

"The Jewish state comes to an end in 70 AD, when the Romans begin to actively drive Jews from the home they had lived in for over a millennium, but the Jewish Diaspora (dispersion, scattering) had begun long before the Romans had even dreamed of Judaea. When Nebuchadnezzar deported the Judaeans in 597 and 586 BC, he allowed them to remain in a unified community in Babylon. Another group of Judaeans fled to Egypt, where they settled in the Nile delta. So from 597 onwards, there were three distinct groups of Hebrews: a group in Babylon and other parts of the Middle East, a group in Judaea, and another group in Egypt. Thus, 597 is considered the beginning date of the Jewish Diaspora. Then, after Jesus was crucified, The Romans then destroyed Jerusalem and systematically drove the Jews from Palestine. After 73 AD, Hebrew history would only be the history of the diaspora as the Jews and their world view spread over Africa, Asia, and Europe" (*Ancient Jewish History: The Diaspora*).

Spread over Africa... Many African-Americans have their roots in Jewish history and it is all thanks to the diaspora. Would it not make sense for when the Good News of Christ began to spread throughout the lands surrounding Israel after his death, for the apostles to first travel to the lands where they already had Jewish ancestry? That was the original order! Matthew 10:5, *"Do not go to the Gentiles or Samaritans, Only The Lost Sheep of Israel."* 1 Peter Chapter 1will show his travels all over. Phillip went to Samaria and Ethiopia (Acts 8). The Messiah is always welcome in Africa. The Diaspora was a blessing in disguise; making The Messiah an easier "sell"? Now, I hope to sell The Messiah to all who believe or who are willing too.

Jehovah's Witnesses are really no different than any Christian denomination. One difference besides the name is that they are the most equally racially divided denomination among Christians! The other is Jehovah. Jehovah is a kind of hybrid English/Hebrew word for our God. The Original -Written- Name was YHWH because there was no vowels in ancient Hebrew so it was up to the reader to pronounce it: it was pronounced Yahweh or Yahuweh or Yehovah and many more, all considering on the reader. The Y has a J sounding flow to it, but the letter J didn't exist until the 13th century. YHWH was the Root of Jehovah. Sound it out. I've said He has many names. Jehovah is God's original -distinct- name, it is more original than "God" itself. Some Hebrews say He has 7 names -and remember- God never said His name was God, not once! After the Old Testament was completed, some Jews thought it was wrong to speak His original name because It is so sacred. So it was substituted with God or Lord...

Jehovah means "To Become." It was His original name along with "I Am" (Exodus 3:14) because *He Just Is.* Yahweh/Jehovah is His distinct name. You can find Yahweh and Jehovah in the footnotes of modern Bibles for Exodus 3:15.

Jesus is also a hybrid English/Hebrew word. His name was Yehoshua then shortened to Yeshua. Which means "Deliverance" and "Savior." So why do they come knocking on our doors? Because that is what Jesus Christ and the Apostles did, they did it publicly and door to door... Jehovah's Witnesses are just old school. They're just doing what they are supposed to do.

"But You Were My Witnesses, O Israel! Says Jehovah. And You
Are My Servant." (Isaiah 43:10)

More on the Jehovahs can be found on JW.org and JWFacts.com
The Apostles' histories after Christ can be found all
throughout *The Book of Acts* in your Bible. The Jewish Diaspora
explains how we have African Rooted Jews and Christians and
African Rooted Christians that still carry those Jewish roots in
with their doctrines, especially with the use of the Star of David
because of their relation to the Tribe of Judah.

JAH! RASTAFARI, Ever Living-Ever Faithful!

The Rastafari started in the 1930s when Ethiopia elected
the Emperor Haile Selassie. Ras means (Head) and Tafari was
Selassie's first name which means to be revered. Just how the
Pope changes his given name; the Ethiopian Coptics do the same.
The Coptics are one of the closest to the roots of Christianity,
and the Catholic Church has recently made a communion with the
Coptics. JAH comes from a shortened word for God in Hebrew,
Yahweh. In German it was Jahweh. I told you God has many
names. Yah or Jah, it's all language interpretation. This is how
things work on earth, by way of The Tower of Babel.

They believed Selassie was the second coming of Christ,
because of the Prophesy in Zephaniah 3:10-17: "My scattered
people from who live beyond the rivers of Ethiopia. For the Lord will
remove his hand of judgment and will disperse the armies of your
enemy. And the Lord Himself, the King of Israel, will live among you!"

Also, Selassie was given 38 titles, all taken from The
Bible during his inauguration like: "King of Kings," "The
Anointed One," "The Conquering Lion of the Tribe of Judah the
Author of Mankind." Jesus is from The Tribe of Judah and from
the bloodline of King David, which is where Selassie hails from
by way of Menilik I, the son of Solomon and Queen of Sheba. His
name means Son of The Wise, like Solomon's wisdom. This

being about 400 years before the Jewish Diaspora. Selassie was The Truth. His legacy was humble and loving. Selassie never admitted to being the reincarnation of Christ, but when he visited Jamaica, he did not want to upset anyone therefore letting the Rastafari, "Have their way with him."

Rastafari believe Zion is a physical place, Ethiopia, where mankind was birthed. Zion is also a mental state, away from materialism, greed, and the vanity of Babylon. Babylon is western society or any society for that matter, that adheres to the evils of the lower side of mankind. They believe the west has been convoluted from the true origins of how we are suppose to be. They believe in The Bible, but also believe that it was convoluted by western society. Just like most of us do!

Marijuana, the herb, ganja, kaya; like God- it has many names. The Herb is used to assist in mediation and religious devotion. And, they back it up by Biblical verses: Genesis 1:11, Genesis 1:29, Genesis 3:18, Psalms 104:14, Proverbs 15:17, Revelation 22:2.

Bob Marley said, "Marijuana teaches you about yourself." This is why I believe many experience paranoia. Other than actual paranoia, we are afraid of our sub-conscious, our inner truths and false fears. Marijuana can be a good psychologist, I still attest that cleanliness is next to Godliness, but to each their own. For some, marijuana is the ultimate healer. But, if you have used it your whole life for recreation, it is good to clean yourself out to see if it really is best for you. You'd be surprised how good sobriety feels. A marijuana dependency can give you anxiety, a short temper, pure laziness, and not to mention an unhealthy diet because it lowers your blood sugar which causes the sugar cravings. One must be smart enough to know yourself.

(More on Rastafari and Haile Selassie can be found on The New World Encyclopedia)

The Rastafari, like Christians, take much from the Hebrews and like many are ignorant of, they love Jesus Christ. Why are we separating ourselves from each other? We should all be partying together! Take part in each others' customs to Praise Jah, Allah, Yahweh, Jehovah, Eloheim, Elyon, EL... God.

"Sing, O Daughter of Zion; Shout Aloud, O Israel. Be Glad and Rejoice With All Your Heart, O Daughter of Jerusalem!" (Zephaniah 3:14)

I sat down next to her and then I noticed she had tears in her eyes. I asked why and she just said, she was tired... I had to call her out on this. But, then I ask where she's from cause I didn't recognize her accent, she tells me Ethiopia and she's been here since 2009. I immediately say, "Oh wow are you Coptic? The Copts are the closest on earth to the real truth of any current Christian religion, Have you been to a coptic church out here?" She tells me every now and then but it is not a Coptic Church, so I try to find one for her, as I ask why she's so tired...

She tells me she's a single mother raising a 6 year old son alone, I said, "Oh no, he doesn't shut up does he?" She starts laughing. She begins to tell me she can raise the boy alone, she's saying this knowing she can't, it just comes off like that. I explain to her how important a Father is to a man because a mother can't always teach a boy all there is to know about being a man, "Listen my Mom is tough as hell and comes from a tough family with 6 brothers, and there was still a lot I had to figure out on my own, and trust me that is usually a recipe for many hard lessons. Chances are the kid will feel somewhat feminine and end up gravitating towards trouble so he feels more masculine... 2Pac shared this openly, also Kanye West."

Then I found the church, there actually was a Coptic Church in Denver, and she was very surprised for being still "tired." As she prepared to leave the train, as I had to stay, she thanked me over and over and over. I thought about getting her information but I didn't want to ruin it. She's a woman who lost hope in men and it happens for all of us sometimes, but it is because people are so superficial and foundations can be weak.

I'm hoping she finds her future husband in that Coptic Church.

"There is a Coptic church in Ethiopia that is said to be housing the Ark of the Covenant. The Ark holds the two stone tablets that the 10 Commandments were written on and holds the Power of God. Menelik, son of King Solomon and the Queen of Sheeba, is said to have brought the Ark to Ethiopia after coming to see his father in Jerusalem when he reached maturity. The Ark is said to be housed now at the Church of Our Lady Mary of Zion. (*Keepers of the Lost Ark?*).

The Copts of Egypt invented Monasticism in Christianity, the complete disregard of worldly pursuits to pursue only spiritual work, we know them as Monks. It was Saint Anthony the Great that started this. After his parents passed away when he was 18, he gave some of the inherited property to neighbors, sold the rest and gave the funds raised to the poor and pursued a life following Christ. During the last persecutions of the followers of Christ in the Roman empire in the year 311, called the Diocletianic, Anthony returned to Alexandria with ambitions to martyr himself for the imprisoned Christians. He fought openly in public for them hoping to be killed, but he was not. After the persecutions he returned back to his "spot" and the number of his disciples grew after word of his Faith spread. Thus spawning the Christian Monk (*St. Anthony*)."

I love the Copts. Coptic means Egyptian. They were one of the first, if not the first, church devoted to Christ. Mark the Evangelist brought The Good News to Alexandria, Egypt. It was the Apostle Peter that brought Mark on and although Mark's gospel made the New Testament, he was not an apostle, he would listen to the sermons of Peter and was handpicked by our first "Pope." But, Mark's contributions cannot be overlooked! He kicked some ass in Africa. "Mark founded the church of Alexandria in Egypt." The Copts were among the first Christian churches of the world which of course was first rooted in Jerusalem directly after the sacrifice of Christ and then spread by the Apostles, which may I remind everyone, were Hebrew.

Remember though, The Original Followers of Christ had NO RELIGION. They still participated in Hebrew Traditions. The Last Supper was actually a Passover meal, "My time has come and I will eat the Passover meal at your house (Matthew 26:18)." Religion is man-made and causes separation between cultures although at the same time it does bring a oneness inside each culture. I believe in the distant or maybe in even the near future we will all have one identity as a religion through the Holy Spirit. As long as we are living in a material world though, people will always try to put you in a box, give you a label. If you are anything like myself, you are somewhat of an existentialist. You despise titles, just like one of my idols, Bob Dylan. But, I just gave us a title didn't I? It just means we prefer to be as authentic as possible according to our own Gospel's of Truth. However, there is a root to your truth, and that is God. God lives within us and although God is complex, It is very simple... Just Love Everyone, Do Unto Others as You Would Have Them Do Unto You, and Praise God.

*But, what does do unto others as you would have them do unto you really mean? I have to thank the great Immanuel Kant for the help on this one. If say, you "love" sleeping with other women, then for sure the woman is allowed to do the same. No cheating without permission, but good luck with that, you know you are no swinger. It is still possible to live in Peace by not following stereotypical moral codes. Just don't get married, because then cheating is completely against the rules, no question. That is adultery through and through. You can also relate this to many things, like "busting chops." Some say it's mean, but not if the other person is game. And usually, no one is game when You Dig Deep. Keep it light hearted, don't go for the jugular man.

You should listen to *Can You Get to That* by Funkadelic. That is my Golden Rule song and What a Groove!
How about some more Kant? I just Kant help myself...
"Since we OUGHT to realize the highest good. That we OUGHT to implies we can. We CAN realize it only if God Exists."

Since it's all of our Duties to realize The Truth, it means We Can BE our best, if we know God exists. Those values of good can only come from GOD. God's Law Trumps All. If you say you can still be Good without God, you May not be wrong, you just don't realize that those morals you follow were actually invented by God. By believing in God, you have a Root. Root can't be broken if you Respect It. Having a True Belief in God gives us the notion that True Love Exists, so we OUGHT to Find It by Acting On It.

***I Kant Help Myself

"Seek not the favor of the multitude; it is seldom got by honest and lawful means. But seek the testimony of few; and number not voices, weigh them." (This sounds like Politics vs. Religion to me, which sounds more authentic?)
"I had therefore to remove knowledge, in order to make room for belief." (Kant knew he was being *Too Smart)
"Thoughts without content are empty. Intuition without concepts are blind." (Ignorance)
"Morality is not properly the doctrine of how we may make ourselves happy, but how we may make ourselves worthy of Happiness." (For The Truest of Hearts)
"If the Truth shall kill them, let them die."
"A single line in The Bible has consoled me more than all the books I ever read."
"You only know me as you see me, not as I am."
"All our knowledge begins with the senses, proceeds then to the understanding, and ends with reason. There is nothing higher than reason."
"All perception is colored by Emotion."
"The only thing permanent is change."
"One is not rich by what one owns, but by what one is able to do without, with dignity."
"I am an investigator by inclination. I feel a great thirst for knowledge."
"There are two things that don't have to mean anything: Music and Laughter."
"Most men only use their knowledge under the guidance from others, because they lack the courage to think independently using their own reasoning abilities. It takes intellectual daring to discover The Truth."

"When I could have used a wife, I could not support one; and when I could support one, I no longer needed any."
"The existence of The Bible as a Book for the people, is the greatest benefit which the human race has ever experienced. Every attempt to belittle it is a crime against humanity!"

     The Bible and all the books of the religions were really the first books on psychology and social work. Every idea from psychology and social work is rooted from the religions. They were the *First books written, period. *The Vedas* in India, *Egyptian Book of the Dead*, and *The Sumerian Tablets* all came around the same time, about 1600 BC give or take a hundred years or so, coincidence? The Torah, The Bible, The Qur'an, The Bhagavad Gita all stems from the Sumerians, Egyptians, and Vedas. There is a lot to research here that you can do on your own, thanks to the internet making it much easier for us, but I am here to bring people together! For example here is my Holy Trinity...

THE HOLY TRINITY***
I AM, Jehovah, Elohim, Brahma, God, Our Rock,
Jesus Christ, Krishna, Lord Shiva...
El Elyon, Lord Vishnu, Allah, God, God The Most High, The Holy Spirit, The God of The Universe, The Redeemer, That Essence, The Substance, THE BIG ? No One Knows What IT Is!

     Notice the first Hebrew word El Elyon. That is Hebrew for "God The Most High." Elyon on its own means: most high, up high, in the heavens, in the sky, and also God. They say this word, Elyon, is where we got Alien from. Sound it out, Elyon, Alien. All Alien means is not from earth. Stop picturing a gray skinny creature in your heads. I think we are from there, or some of us are. Not everyone has a soul. You know the Hebrews have different DNA than the rest of the white race? Are we from Orion or the Pleiades or anywhere The Lord created?

    "Can you hold back the movements of the stars? Are you able to restrain the Pleiades or loosen the bands of Orion?" (Job 38:31)

"He made all the stars: the Bear, Orion, the Pleiades, and the constellations of the southern sky (Job 9:9)."

But like I said, I am here to bring people together, not rocket us to outer space. Where we really came from is really all up in the air, but it is fun to theorize. What is important now, is getting back to The Roots of religion. If religions cannot get along, then no one can. Religion and science should be getting along too. God is science. God is All Things. Even Albert Einstein said,

"The more I study science, the more I believe in God."

"I believe in Spinoza's God, who reveals Himself in the lawful harmony of the world, not in a God that concerns Himself with the fate and the doings of mankind."

"A knowledge of the existence of something we cannot penetrate, of the manifestations of the profoundest reason and the most radiant beauty - it is this knowledge and this emotion that constitute the truly religious attitude; in this sense, and in this alone, I am a deeply religious man."

How could something so magnificent be just from chance? Something is going on that we may never explain. The Big Bang is a Theory. It is called the Big Bang *Theory* right? It was an explosion. It was a bomb, but something has to make a bomb for it to be set off right? And why does Venus (The Morning Star) Spin Backwards? An asteroid made it spin the other way? That is what scientists say. That does not seem very Big Bang like does it? I am not here to debate science though. One cannot mess with Einstein though. If you want more information on science, from a NASA employee that came to believe in God after thorough research then go here: *The Solar System and What You Are Not Being Told About Astronomy FULL* VIDEO. https://www.youtube.com/watch?v=ng-OQBaHcWg

To make something out of nothing is Art. Science is the study of what is already there. Hmmm, "*Our Father who Art in Heaven.*"

And that is how you pray, Jesus said in Matthew 6:5-13,

"Don't be like the hypocrites who pray openly for everyone to see them. When you pray go away by yourself and pray secretly. Do not babble on and on like the pagan's do. Don't be like them for Your Father already knows what you need even before you ask Him! Pray like this,

"Our Father who Art in Heaven,
Hallowed be thy name, thy Kingdom come, thy will be done,
On Earth as it is in Heaven, Give us this day our daily bread,
And forgive us our trespasses,
As we forgive those who trespass against us,
And lead us not into temptation, but deliver us from evil."

Can an atheist get in to Heaven? That depends on what made that person not believe, I believe. Also, what knowledge they have. In our current world there is no way ignorance is forgiven without some punishment considering we have every piece of information ever at our fingertips. Ignorance is a sin. Jesus did however say, "Forgive them Father for they know not what they do." But what if we can easily know what we do?

~Paradigm Shift of the Smart Phone~

Everything on earth and in the stars has a higher purpose and all the answers for the mysteries are in Each Religion's books and the Apocryphal Books that were not allowed in them at that time. They would have most likely been allowed in now. People did not evolve yet to hear certain truths and the people running the show have not evolved either... Although many still haven't. Some like to use the fact that the verses in all the books should not be taken literally, therefore it is false. It is called poetry! Here is an example in Ezekiel 3:3,

"The voice said to me, 'Son of man, eat what I am giving you- eat this scroll! Then go and give its message to the people of Israel.' So I opened my mouth and he fed me the scroll. 'Eat it all,' he said. And when I ate it, it tasted as sweet as honey."

Now did Ezekiel really eat paper? Maybe! We cannot sit

here and just read a verse like this and say that is crazy, plus we were not there! You telling me that you never had a kid in your class growing up that didn't chew paper? We all know that person. The other side of this was that Ezekiel actually read the scroll, ingested it like the Lamb of God. We really do not need food, all we need is The Word of God,
"When your words came, I ate them; they sustain me. They bring me great joy and are my heart's delight, for I bear your name, O Lord God Almighty." (Jeremiah 15:16)

Another argument, some say Religion is ONLY to control people? What a cop out! Hey the Police are here to control us too, do we not put our faith in them for our protection? There is no safety and comfort like that of the Almighty, "Because you have seen, you believed, but Blessed are those who believe without seeing." (John 20:29)

I do agree, religion is here to control people, absolutely, but that is because one reason, we needed it! The Bible and other Books would have read much different if we were good boys and girls. Duh! All it would have said was, "I Love You, You Love Me, We're a Happy Family." Yes I quoted *Barney*, because that is how simple it is! We are all suppose to be like children to enter heaven (Matthew 18:3). Instead we got thousands of pages and we still don't get IT. There are contradictions in the Bible of some laws because of our free will. We evolve, we digress, we evolve, we digress and I've used this source before (Matthew 19:8) straight from Christ Himself, to prove how man compromises during our evolution even when it is not how God originally intended it to be. Typical of us to point the finger instead of looking at ourselves. If there was no compromise, God wouldn't exist in this world! When God doesn't exist here, He takes "Here" away.

Here's another one, "I could have easily wrote The Bible." Yeah sure. These people have never even read it! And, couldn't pass English Comp I. The ignorance in some people is so ridiculous. They have no idea how intelligent it is. One cannot make up those historical stories! And it is thorough. And Wise.

And Loving. You cannot write Love and Wisdom like that. They know nothing about Love and Wisdom. If they did, they wouldn't have said something as arrogant as, "I could write The Bible." No they can't, who are they kidding? These lessons are not from here. These lessons are also ***Timeless. One can read the same passage two or three times and come to two or three different conclusions at different time periods because that is how intelligent it is! Timeless like Bob Dylan.

So, why didn't Jesus write for Himself? IT is all instincts for him, IT oozed out of him. God and The Prophets are all heart. This is most likely why Jesus hired Matthew, the tax collector, to be his realistic detail oriented recorder. While the Artistic Apostle John took care of the metaphysical side. Mark and Luke weren't there during the 3 years of Christ's ministry. Mark wrote his words from Peter's sermons and Luke was like a news reporter, both after the death of Christ. BUT: Phillip, Thomas, James, Judas, Peter, and Mary were all there! And you could find them in the Nag Hammadi Scriptures and The Dead Sea Scrolls. Also The Buddha didn't write. The Vedas were written by Sages and Sages also wrote Krishna's Bhagavad Gita. John the Baptist didn't write, he was all instincts baby. It is also said that Aaron did more speaking (if not all) than his younger brother Moses as well. (Exodus 4:10-17, 5:1-13, 6:10-13, 6:28-7:7). Elijah didn't write and several other Prophets of Old this applies to. Hard to remember your instincts. Plus, how can one write their own story? Especially concerning Godly work. You need vouchers.

The stubborn believe that a life with God is -only- a choice out of desperation. Some do choose this for that reason, and that's great! But others, like myself, had a mixture of both. I Figured IT Out. This took many years of studying with Belief and Disbelief. Did I carry guilt with me also? Of course, there was underlying desperation, my life had some traumas, but I am not going to choose anything because of guilt. I have to figure it out intellectually and pretty sure I have proven that. I hope I have helped you do the same. Do not take my words for it. Go study for yourself, there is so much more to learn! I just wanted to plant the root! All you have to do nowadays is just type in your question instead of reading every book! I hope I made this book an easy experience, but I am not done yet, almost there... If we are the desperate ones why do they, who scorn us, choose: drugs, alcohol, vanity, greed, gluttony, pride, and promiscuous sex to "heal?" Is it even Healing? Doubt it. I don't need anything but: music, literature, exercise, macaroni, and sleep. So who is really desperate? And why do they not feel guilty for those selfish sometimes vulgar acts?

"Blessed are you when people hate you, when they exclude you and insult you and reject your name as evil, because of The Son of Man. Rejoice in that day and leap for joy. Because great is your reward in Heaven. For that is how their ancestors treated the Prophets."
(Luke 6:22-23)

"If anyone acknowledges me publicly here on earth, I will openly acknowledge that person before my Father in Heaven. But if anyone denies me here on earth, I will deny that person before my Father in Heaven." (Matthew 10:32-33)

"If the people of the village won't receive your message when you enter it, shake off its dust from your feet as you leave. It is a sign that you have abandoned that village to its fate." (Luke 9:5)

"As for you, be as shrewd as snakes and as innocent as doves."
(Matthew 10:16)

Why can't we accept that some people can't follow certain paths of life? It's not up to them, it's up to you. Why do your closest friends not let you be your own? Why do you have to say bye to them just to do this? Do not try to change them, give them your root, your truth, and if they do not ask more, move on. You cannot change the heart of the stubborn, they have to come into it on their own. Place your love elsewhere perhaps. And:

"Don't do your good deeds publicly, to be admired, because then you will lose the reward from your Father in Heaven" (Matthew 6:1).

You can always tell whose a Godly person when they donate anonymously, sometimes they don't even believe in God, but what they don't know is that God invented that. God invented every righteous thing on this planet, yet no one gives credit when credit is due. By helping others, you're helping yourself, but if your motivation is to help yourself... It does not apply.

"You can't love someone unless you love yourself." This is bullshit. Why? Well for one this quote is from a human perspective not a spiritual one. Loving yourself borders on vanity. We are suppose to be selfless. Completely selfless is the way into heaven.

"The absence of awareness robs your body of the wealth of spirituality. This absence of awareness is created by your own ignorance. If you wash off that ignorance with the energy of will, then where does the possibility of the absence of Awareness exist?" Lord Shiva

That is the true essence of the Holy Spirit. Leave yourself alone! It is not easy to have this kind of self-awareness, but it is possible. Leave yourself alone. They say the grass isn't always greener on the other side or "That wherever you go there you are." Well I am saying, depending on where you came from, your history, and the people you are surrounded by; it can be best to get your ass out of dodge. Just because you sinned yesterday does not mean you can't run with it today! John the Baptist is the man to see,

"Who is this man you went out to see in the wilderness? What did you expect to see? Did you find him weak as reed? Moved by every breath of wind? You do not see Fine Clothing in the Wilderness. Expensive clothes are only in Palaces. Were you looking for a Prophet? Yes, and He is more than a Prophet!"
***Luke 7:18-35 & Matthew 11:1-19

Do you know what the most important thing on Earth is to God? It's your Soul. He wants to mush the living heck out of it.
He Can If You Believe!

"The concept of Imagination is perhaps the most important key to the understanding of the Opus" Carl Jung

"The man who never in his mind and thoughts traveled to heaven is no Artist" William Blake

Being noticed by or noticing God... the answer is evidence, there is evidence all around us in the laws of nature and in books. There's no books on grape heads, right? If it is just a form of escapism, why is there: evidence, history, and clear signs. We can imagine anything, we all know this, but this doesn't mean God isn't real. Magnets, lights, sound, and People all have an Aura around them that we can't see but we know it is there... God's Aura is Everywhere. Feeling and Seeing God is through Imagination by way of our Hearts. I hope I helped you open up your heart. Now use that imagination. Do not try to imagine, just let your Faith take control of you. Receive It! Be a Vessel!

"Once Meek and in a Perilous Path, The Just Man Kept His Course Along The Vale Of Death, Roses are Planted Where Thorns Grow and on the Barren Heath, Sing the Honey Bees"

William Blake from The Marriage of Heaven and Hell

"Believe Me, The Sun is as The Flame of a Candle Beside The Sun of Truth of the Heavenly Father"

Jesus Christ from The Essene Gospel of Peace

"I Baptize with Water for Repentance so that you can turn to God, but who comes after me, Baptizes with The Holy Spirit and Fire. And he will come with his winnowing fork to burn the chaff with never-ending fire" John THE Baptist (Matthew 3:11-12)

"The Light of Our Eyes The Hearing of Our Ears, Both are Born of The Colours and The Sounds of Our Earthly Mother"

Jesus Christ

May The Holy Spirit Bless Your Soul

REFERENCES

The Holy Bible. New Living Translation, Gift and Award Edition. Tyndale House Publishers, Inc. 1997.

The Nag Hammadi Scriptures. The International Edition. Edited by Marvin Meyer. 2007.

The Bhagavad Gita. Vyasa. Translated from the Sanskrit by Swami Nikhilananda. New York Ramakrishna-Vivekananda Center. 1944.

The Vedas. Single Volume, Unabridged. Translations by Ralph T. H. Griffith and Arthur Berriedale Keith. Kshetra Books. 2017.

The Noble Qur'an. A summarized version of At-Tabari, Al-Qurtubi and Ibn Kathir. Maktaba Darussalam. 1996.

The Essene Gospel of Peace. Translated from the Aramaic Manuscript by Edmond Bordeaux Szekely. Academy of Creative Living. 1971.

He Walked the Americas. L. Taylor Hansen. Ray Palmer, Legend Press. 1963.

Religion. Mayan, Incan, Aztec. http://mayaincaaztec.com. Accessed March 2017.

Quetzalcoatl. http://www.crystalinks.com/quetzalcoatl.html. Accessed March 2017.

The Gospel of the Toltecs. Frank Diaz. Bear & Company. 2002.

Haile Selassie. New World Encyclopedia. 6 Aug 2016, 20:57 UTC. 26 Mar 2017, 20:07 <http://www.newworldencyclopedia.org/p/index.php? title=Haile_Selassie&oldid=998446>.

Who were The Essenes. Excerpted from The Essenes and The Lessons by Olivier Manitara. http://www.essenespirit.com/who.html.

Accessed March 2017.

Doctrine One. Doctrines of the Modern Essene Church. Rev. Brother Day, High Priest. http://www.essene.org/Essene_Doctrine.htm#D4. Accessed March 2017.

Ancient Jewish History: The Diaspora. Richard Hooker. https://www.jewishvirtuallibrary.org/the-diaspora. Accessed March 2017.

St. Anthony. Edward Cuthbert Buter. The Catholic Encyclopedia. Vol. 1. New York: Robert Appleton Company, 1907. 26 http://www.newadvent.org/cathen/01553d.htm. Accessed March 2017.

The Church of Alexandria. Joseph Woods. The Catholic Encyclopedia. Vol. 1. New York: Robert Appleton Company, 1907. 26 http://www.newadvent.org/cathen/01300b.htm. Accessed March 2017

Keepers of the Lost Ark? Paul Raffaele. Smithsonian Mag. Dec 2007. http://www.smithsonianmag.com/travel/keepers-of-the-lost-ark-179998820/. Accessed March 2017.

YHWH- Jehovah or Yahweh. Paul Grundy. http://www.jwfacts.com/watchtower/jehovah-yahweh.php. Accessed March 2017

Who is Jehovah. https://www.jw.org/en/bible-teachings/questions/who-is-jehovah/. March, 2017

The Book of Enoch. Translated from the Ethiopian by R.H. Charles, 1906. Saltheart Publishers, LLC. 2013.

Book of Mormon. "Origins." https://www.mormonwiki.com/Book_of_Mormon. Accessed March 2017.

Mormon Polygamy. https://www.mormonwiki.com/%22Mormon %22_Polygamy. Accessed March 2017.

Buddhism. Donald Lopez.https://www.britannica.com/topic/Buddhism. Accessed March 2017.

For: My Darling Babe
Everything I Do: Is, Was, and Always Will Be... For You.

Never Forget Babe,

I Love You

www.ingramcontent.com/pod-product-compliance
Lightning Source LLC
Chambersburg PA
CBHW020514030426
42337CB00011B/390